KU-175-035

The Cycling
ANTHOLOGY

VOLUME ONE

Edited by
Ellis Bacon
&
Lionel Birnie

YELLOW JERSEY PRESS
LONDON

Published by Yellow Jersey Press 2014

2 4 6 8 10 9 7 5 3 1

First published in Great Britain in 2012 by
Peloton Publishing

Yellow Jersey Press
Random House, 20 Vauxhall Bridge Road,
London SW1V 2SA

www.vintage-books.co.uk

Addresses for companies within The Random House Group Limited can be
found at: www.randomhouse.co.uk/offices.htm

The Random House Group Limited Reg. No. 954009

A CIP catalogue record for this book
is available from the British Library

ISBN 9780224092449

The Random House Group Limited supports the Forest Stewardship
Council® (FSC®), the leading international forest-certification organisation.
Our books carrying the FSC label are printed on FSC®-certified paper.
FSC is the only forest-certification scheme supported by the
leading environmental organisations, including Greenpeace.
Our paper procurement policy can be found at:
www.randomhouse.co.uk/environment

Printed in Great Britain by Clays Ltd, St Ives plc

THE CYCLING ANTHOLOGY

THE CYCLING ANTHOLOGY

THE NEUTRALISED ZONE

INTRODUCTION BY THE EDITORS

Thank you for buying this first volume in a series of anthologies that we hope will evolve into a long-lasting and well-loved collection of books.

Professional cycling is such a rich, dynamic and, yes, controversial sport that it lends itself perfectly to the written word. Indeed, many of the great races were founded by newspapermen.

We believe passionately in great writing and so we invited some of the best in the business to contribute to this debut collection.

The idea was to present something we hope will appeal to people who enjoy reading. We're delighted with the final result and are confident there's something to suit all tastes.

We'd like to thank all the writers for making the book a reality and our readers for giving it a try.

We hope you enjoy it and that you'll look forward to our Tour de France special edition next time.

Ellis Bacon & Lionel Birnie

1

William Fotheringham has followed the development of Bradley Wiggins more closely than most.

The Londoner completed his transformation from track star to Tour de France superstar in the summer of 2012.

So, how did he do it?

PROJECT WIGGINS

BY WILLIAM FOTHERINGHAM

Hindsight is a wonderful thing but one little speech from Rod Ellingworth during the 2010 Tour de France is worth revisiting.

The Sky race coach spoke in the middle of a Tour which was viewed as a disaster for a team with the aspirations of the big-budget British squad.

Ellingworth was thinking long-term, beyond the team's debut Tour where Bradley Wiggins was failing to perform a leader's role on or off the bike, when he told me: 'In a business, the building period is 18 months from when you start, so that means two Tours. By the third we should be bang-on.'

How right he was. By the end of the summer of 2012, Sky had turned into the winningest outfit in the game, with a dominant Tour de France behind them.

Wiggins had been converted from a Tour hopeful with one great ride to his name – not even Wiggins himself could work out whether that was a fluke – into a model of consistency, with a perfect curve of performance improvement over two years, taking him from third place at Paris-Nice in 2010 to the gold medal in the time trial at the Olympics.

It was a sporting triumph, but it raised some unexpected issues that would take time to resolve. Wiggins's athletic ability had been tested, but so too his capacity to answer the questions about doping that come with any Tour victory in the era post-Armstrong, Landis and company.

The ethics of Tour winners are no longer taken for granted; Wiggins came to understand that, and duly responded. As he said after the Tour, he doesn't like having to proclaim his probity in public, but he knows he has no option.

After the publication of the United States Anti-Doping Agency's report into Armstrong, belief in the probity of professional cyclists is in short supply. I firmly believe Wiggins won the Tour clean. I base that on knowing the man for 10 years, having seen more of him one to one than I have most other cyclists, having discussed doping with him on many occasions, having a good chance to mull over his body language and his answers, and being in a position to contrast how he talks and acts compared to the dopers I have seen, interviewed and listened to over many years: Armstrong, Vinokourov, Landis, Hamilton, Riis, Pantani, Millar.

Post-Tour, the questions continued concerning members of the Team Sky entourage linked to the Armstrong scandal unveiled by USADA. Even if the individuals concerned – Sean Yates and Michael Rogers – were not directly accused of doping within the report, it was clear from sources within Sky that a response of some kind was in the pipeline after Dave Brailsford's policy of zero tolerance towards those caught up in doping scandals had been proven to have its limits.

The chances were that would involve, at the least, a beefing-up of the policy, and changes in personnel. But that is in the longer-term. The eventual fall-out for Sky remains an open book.

As Armstrong went down in flames, the question that had been forgotten was this: how did Bradley Wiggins win the Tour de France?

Not as in, how did the side-burned superstar of British sport get from Liège to Paris between June 29 and July 22 in the quickest possible time? That's fairly clear.

He did that by not missing a beat in those 23 days; straightforward, if not simple: he stayed upright in the first week, he won the time trials, he climbed the mountains ahead of the others.

The back story merited a good long look, however: no Tour winner had done it in quite the way he did. And at a time when the way cyclists win the Tour had been called into the sharpest possible question, the background mattered as much as the victory itself.

Unlikely as it may sound to those who accompanied him in the *gruppetto* in his first two Tours, Wiggins was a stage racer waiting to be unleashed: this was a rider who had won a mountain stage at the Tour de l'Avenir, who had won the Flèche du Sud in Luxembourg at the ripe old age of 19.

Three episodes from his time in the *gruppetto* Tours spring to mind: 2006, when he wrote that in his first Tour he was waking up fresh and alert in the final week; 2007, when he told me of riding up the Col de l'Iséran in the front group, without really meaning to (before dropping back to his usual place in the *autobus*), and again in 2007, at the stage start in Pau, when he was discussing his high placing in the Albi time trial, deep into the race.

'I didn't know I was that good,' he said. He may have dreamed as a child of emulating his hero Miguel Indurain, but it never crossed his radar.

'He had so much potential in road races when he turned senior,' says Rob Hayles, his former Madison partner who raced with him for Great Britain on the road. 'He could read a race, follow it, get in the moves, but he had years when he switched off.'

There is another critical point: incredible as it sounds, Wiggins says he didn't learn to train until 2011. He is backed up in that by his long-standing mentor Shane Sutton, who laments that 'one of the things he said to me is that he never really trained and he regretted it. We've never seen the real Brad in all those six Olympic medals. Think of the records that could have fallen... but he didn't apply himself as well as he could'.

Why, you might ask, was he 'undertrained', and why did he have no awareness of his potential on the road, when he came out of the immensely analytical, scientific culture at British Cycling?

The answer is that that culture was simultaneously the making of him as he is today, while being a brake on any aspirations Wiggins might have had in road racing. Those could not have been furthered by the timed-discipline, track-only culture that was founded by Peter Keen. Wiggins's coach of eight years (1998-2006) Simon Jones concedes that the Tour was never on their radar. I suspect Wiggins feels that's just as well, given the culture of the needle and the blood bag that was rampant in European road racing in the early noughties. As he has said, the fact he had his speciality on the track to fall back on meant that he never had to make the choice that presented itself to a talented, aspiring road star such as David Millar.

Road racing only became a part of British Cycling's armoury after 2004 when Rod Ellingworth founded the under-23 academy. Prior to that, how a British Cycling track rider performed on the road simply didn't matter. What counted was getting Olympic medals on the track, in the timed events, at the races that mattered in order to secure funding: the World Championships and the Olympic Games. The road was seen purely as a means of building a foundation of fitness to support the intense blocks of track training that were necessary for the individual or team pursuit.

That had several implications. None of the trainers at British Cycling thought of making their best pursuiter lose weight and ride through the Alps and Pyrenees with the best climbers to see where they stood in the road hierarchy – but why would they? It wasn't in their remit. The track endurance riders clearly had the talent to perform on the road, with the possible exception of Ed Clancy, who is more akin to Sir Chris Hoy than he is to your average pursuiter. Even when training for the pursuit, with the bulkier shoulders and backside of a track rider, Wiggins was capable of performing on the road, winning hilly stage races in Luxembourg and Majorca, time trialling over the mountains to win a stage of the Tour de l'Avenir. But no one looked at that.

Hence the lack of training for the road. Up to 2008, the blocks of preparation that Wiggins and his peers were putting in for the track were intense, but they were purely oriented towards performing for a few days, for four to eight minutes a day. There is a world of difference between looking at that and building for the Tour de France, and it's not knowledge that is gained overnight.

What can be traced is an obvious process in which Wiggins spends seven years racing as a pro (2002-2008) on the road, picking up the odd result here and there. All that time, however, when the going gets tough, when he wonders what the opposition are up to after yet another drugs scandal, or when the choice is between training in the rain or doing something more pleasant, he has the fall-back: none of this road stuff matters, because I have to be at my very best in August for the Games or, alternatively, I don't need to do this, because I've just achieved my goal for the year, I've won my medal.

Hence the sporadic results, hence the pattern of aspiration for the road which subsides gently on an almost annual basis. He's supported in this by French pro road racing culture, where he is pigeon-holed as a prologue time trial specialist à la Chris Boardman, as Robert Millar rightly identified: 'For a track rider like Brad in a French team, as he was for so long, all they want is for you to win a prologue time trial. They don't care if you get dropped later in the race. There is no probing, no questioning.'

The view of the other Millar, David, is instructive here. In *Racing Through the Dark* he describes Wiggins as 'a chameleon-like personality: [with] a strong desire to blend in and tell people what they wanted to hear'. Critically here, the people who told Wiggins what to do early on were the track specialists: Jones and Keen. He was capable of finishing in the front group in the road race at the Madrid World Championships in 2005 but, by implication, he was not capable of seeing his own potential outside the track domain, until he had no choice but to broaden his horizons.

At the end of 2008, the comfort blankets are taken away; there is nothing more for Wiggins to achieve on the track after taking two gold medals in Beijing to go with his three medals, one of each colour, in Athens.

Simultaneously, he sees two things going on in the road cycling world: Mark Cavendish – that little fat kid from a few years back to whom he once gave a box of gels at a criterium and who later became his Madison partner – is winning bunch sprints left, right and centre and gaining colossal kudos and a fair bit of cash. And his old mate from the track squad, Steve Cummings – another occasional road racer with Great Britain in the early 2000s – has left the British Cycling nest, dropped a few kilos, and appears to have the makings of a career on the road. If they can do it, why not him?

'It felt like it was a conscious decision,' says his coach at the time, Matt Parker. 'He had done everything he could do to be successful on the track and he made the switch [to road] in his head. He had just come off a two- or three-year Olympic campaign, but he didn't miss a beat that next year. Before, he had continually switched from road to track and back again, but now he didn't have to keep making the transition. He had never been far off it on the road. He had incredible power, and in 2009 he stripped down in terms of weight.'

Wiggins has no idea quite what he is trying to do. He has absolutely no notion what area of road racing he might be good at – apart from the prologues in which he has always excelled – but he gets the kilos off with the help of the British Cycling diet guru Nigel Mitchell and Parker. Between them, they get him light, but at the same time he retains a power output that would give him a 4,000-metre pursuit time not much slower than he would manage at his heaviest on the track. That is the key to his success.

So in 2009, Wiggins tries a bit of everything: a prologue time trial here, pushing for a long time trial there, smashing it in Paris-Roubaix, testing his climbing in the Giro d'Italia. His objectives are undefined, until he gets within a couple of weeks of the 2009 Tour de France. As David Millar wrote, 'Contrary to what Jonathan Vaughters would have people think, we had absolutely no idea he would become a grand tour contender or challenger in anything but the flattest and most simple of stage races.'

Before the start of the 2009 Tour, Wiggins tells me (on condition I don't write it as he thinks people may laugh) that he thinks he might get a top 10 place. I'm sceptical. But Wiggins is lucky, in many, many ways. While he is getting on with his last year on the track, 2008, on the road there has been the latest in a series of clear-outs of dopers in the sport. Riccardo Ricco, Leonardo Piepoli, Bernhard Kohl, and Stefan Schumacher have all been busted for CERA, the latest derivative of the blood-boosting drug EPO. That follows Operation Puerto in 2006 (which claimed Jan Ullrich, Ivan Basso, Joseba Beloki and Francisco Mancebo) and the 'Tour de Farce' of 2007 (which culled Alexandre Vinokourov, Michael Rasmussen and Iban Mayo).

The three years of scandals at the top of the sport means that in 2009, in spite of Lance Armstrong's comeback and Alberto Contador's return to the Tour after being refused entry in 2008, there is space at the summit of the hierarchy given the number of riders who are banned; the ones who have been banned, come back and are now running scared; the ones who are just scared and have stopped. As a further deterrent, the effects of the UCI's biological passport is kicking in. Wiggins's new team, Garmin, have already placed Christian Vande Velde in the higher reaches of the standings in the Tour, and that's precisely what they manage again. The rest is history. Fourth place in the Tour.

* * *

Wiggins brings a lot more to the party than an engine that can put out 450 watts for an hour at threshold. During and after the Tour it became fashionable to dismiss the Londoner as a 'numbers monkey', obsessed with the vital statistics relating to his

training and racing: the 100,000 vertical metres of
climbing he was expected to manage between April
and June – roughly 10,000 per week; the *velocita ascen-
sionale media* [VAM] by which he and Kerrison measure his progress up each climb; the power outputs
he can detail from the time trials he has ridden.

Wiggins has several vital assets, but perhaps
the most important is his ability to learn from his
mistakes. The 2010 season is a wake-up call of epic
proportions: the humiliation of failure – in relative
terms – in the Tour amid epic levels of hype; the
prospect of losing his status and wage when Sky
threaten to demote him at the end of the season; the
brutal reminder of his own mortality after the sudden death of his grandfather, George – the closest
person he has had to a father.

So he recognises a string of errors: approaching
the Tour without specific training, working on the
assumption that what had brought him success
in 2009 would work again; a lack of guidance that
can – from the outside – be put down to the sheer
speed with which Team Sky was built from scratch to
ProTour level. Once he acquires that guidance, in the
form of Tim Kerrison and Shane Sutton, the awareness grows.

The Eureka moment came when Wiggins
finished third in the Vuelta a España in September
2011. Here, two key things happened. Up until then
there had always been a grain of doubt in his mind, a

question mark over the 2009 Tour. Was it a fluke? The doubt was dispelled after he finished on the podium, very close to winning a race which didn't suit him in the slightest – only one time trial, in which he didn't perform at his best, and a plethora of mountain-top finishes – and he did so after six weeks training with a broken collarbone. It could hardly be matched as a confidence booster.

At this point he and his trainer, Kerrison, made the breakthrough. Wiggins had not raced before the Vuelta. He had not turned a pedal in anger since he broke his collarbone in a crash en route to Château-roux in the Tour de France, some six weeks before the Vuelta started. For at least half a century, the received wisdom in cycling has been that riders need to race as part of their training. Suddenly it became apparent that this was not the case.

The discovery goes back to the matter of Wiggins 'never learning to train'. In his years at British Cycling, no one had looked hard at what a rider needed to do in order to win the Tour de France. There was no reason to do that as I've explained. Once Kerrison began looking at Wiggins's 'numbers' – the TrainingPeaks stress scores that express how hard a particular day's work has been – the answers became clear. Conventional wisdom says you train, you back off, you race, you recover. The combination of the taper, travel days and the recovery days means a multiplication of the lost time, with the irony being that in many cases the rider is recovering more from the travel than the actual racing.

In terms of moving forward within a structured training plan, racing can be completely counterproductive. For example, there is no point in riding the Ardennes Classics if your mind is set on the Tour. As Wiggins says, why travel to Liège or Maastricht, spend a week in a hotel to ride Flèche Wallonne and Liège-Bastogne-Liège, to put your body through the mill for two days, when the workload is uncertain and either event is completely open to the vagaries of chance: one crash and that's a week's training down the pan.

Most radical of all was the discovery that as a rider becomes fitter, racing becomes a game of diminishing returns. Once you think about it, it makes perfect sense. You have to train harder, because the racing gets easier, overloads your system less, and thus it is having less of an improving effect. The killer quote from Wiggins's account of his road to Tour victory is this: 'The Dauphiné didn't touch the sides.' It is a remarkable notion: one of the toughest pre-Tour 'preparation' races which actually wasn't that hard.

It's only possible to believe that when this fact is borne in mind: at the Tenerife training camp 10 days out from the Dauphiné, Wiggins and company put in the training equivalent to two weeks of a grand tour, but under conditions controlled by their coach to maximise their benefit and with none of the transfers and general crapping about that make stage racing so stressful.

* * *

If you were setting out to win the Tour de France the Wiggins way, here is what you might do. These aspects of his preparation worked to perfection.

■ Lifestyle. Wiggins went to extremes to maintain a low body weight, avoid injury and avoid illness. That entailed having no sugar, bread or biscuits in the house, walking as little as possible, never so much as putting his suitcase in the car when he left for the airport. Beyond the extremes came a realisation that winning the Tour is a 12-months-a-year exercise. There perhaps lies the ultimate contrast with the track: to hit the ground running in early February, he had to be ready to begin training hard from the first day of November. The upshot was that apart from one cold, Wiggins missed barely a single day's training between November 1 and mid-August. There was no time spent playing catch-up. The programme could be adhered to in its entirety.

■ Start training early and build a massive base. Wiggins set out on his road to the 2012 Tour and Olympic Games on November 1. He had raced to a high level to the end of the 2011 season, finishing the World Championships in fine fettle, and this in turn meant that when he got back on the road – having actually taken time completely away from riding his bike – he was able to ramp up the workload rapidly with no adverse effects. That's why he was able to put in a 40-hour week shortly before Christmas at Sky's training camp in Mallorca; that put him on a par with Edvald Boasson Hagen, one of the team's Classics specialists who was expected to peak far earlier in the season.

■ Training early at intensity so that there is no process of adaptation when racing starts. This came from Tim Kerrison's work in Australian swimming, in which the athletes train at a high level for far longer than in cycling, where the end-of-season break and a gradual build is the norm, with races used to hone fitness. Kerrison turned that on its head: Wiggins began high-intensity work early – although reserving the toughest, longest and most specific sessions for late in the process – and was already close to his best at his first race in early February, the Volta ao Algarve, where he won the time trial. By then he was already close to 95 per cent of his best form, and he built on that until mid-June.

■ Identifying the best venues in which to train. This was a task which Rod Ellingworth had highlighted as important even before Sky's formation, but which Tim Kerrison worked on in 2011. Tenerife was identified as a key location because of the variety of roads on offer, the almost guaranteed good weather, and the relative isolation of the Hotel Parador on the top of Mount Teide. All there is to do there is train and rest. Tenerife was not unknown within cycling, having been used by Lance Armstrong and Alexandre Vinokourov *inter alia*, but tends not to be popular with many teams because the harsh climate means riders need back-up from at least a soigneur and mechanic. Sky travelled with a large group of riders and staff – around a dozen – representing a considerable investment.

■ Using races intelligently. The irony is that Wiggins's plethora of stage race wins – four in one year – owes nothing to the haphazard 'cannibalistic' approach of a Merckx, an Hinault or a Kelly, where the rider consumes every event in sight until his body and mind are sated. Far from it. Under Kerrison and Sutton, the rider is not setting out to win races left, right and centre. The races have a purpose: to rehearse rider and team for the main goal, to ensure that they are used to the entire process of leading a bike race, from defending the lead to having the recovery drinks ready and waiting for the leader to consume in the post-stage press conference.

Winning the races is important, but not to the

extent that training towards the main goal is compromised: the taper is small, the training load maintained as late as possible, training resumed afterwards.

'Traditionally, there is a culture in cycling of racing every week,' said Kerrison. 'We have tried to get back to racing and training, racing less to free up big blocks of time when Brad can train in control of what he does. He has done fewer races, has gone there with the goal of winning, but without going out of his way to prepare for them. If you go to win, mentally you back off, we've preferred not to compromise his training, go there with what we've got.'

■ Preparing everyone around the leaders. Part of Kerrison's plan for Tour success involved the core of the Tour de France team putting in the same preparation as the riders who would lead at the Tour, racing together and training together so they all arrived at the Tour as a tight-knit unit in the form of their lives. The team was built around seven riders known as the climbing group: Wiggins, Chris Froome, Michael Rogers, Kanstantsin Siutsou, Richie Porte, Christian Knees, and Danny Pate, who was ruled out of the race at the last minute. These seven followed a similar programme, participating in the altitude training camps in Tenerife and racing every event alongside Wiggins, with only slight variations. The specific aim was to build a close-knit group with similar capabilities, all able to ride strongly both in the mountains and on the flat. With Edvald Boasson Hagen added for the Critérium du Dauphiné and an obvious selection, that left only the question of who would accompany Mark Cavendish. Sky opted for Bernhard Eisel, who ended up a vital asset in the battle for the yellow jersey, according to Wiggins.

■ Identifying physical weaknesses that need to be worked on. The approach adopted by Kerrison and Sutton involved brutally honest analysis of Wiggins's capabilities. Early in 2011, Kerrison identified that he faltered when he climbed at altitudes over 1,500 metres. The answer was altitude acclimatisation – not the traditional living at altitude to increase red blood cells, but training at race intensity at over 1,500 metres to force his body to adapt.

The Sky leader's relatively poor performance on the Alto del Angliru in the Vuelta a España led to an analysis of his upper body and core strength, which needed improvement. The upshot was a strength and conditioning programme. A similar approach was taken to time trialling: Kerrison examined his time trial style compared to that of Tony Martin and concluded that there was no option but to push a bigger gear at a lower cadence, hence a programme of torque training – big-gear work at threshold.

■ Taking off the pressure. The presences of Mark Cavendish and Chris Froome were disruptive in one way, beneficial in another. Sources within Sky indicate that Cavendish felt he could go for the green jersey; Cavendish himself said he felt he could have won three stages more than the three he did win. The tensions with Froome were obvious and clearly had an impact. But whereas in 2010 and 2011 Wiggins was the sole leader of the team, Cavendish's leadership qualities and his high-profile personality took the pressure off him, in the first week at least. Froome's presence meant that if there was a repeat of the 2011 crash, Sky had a Plan B.

■ Racing to your strengths. It sounds blindingly obvious, but is surprisingly nuanced. One key to the Wiggins Tour of 2012 was the decision by Sutton and Kerrison in the winter of 2010-11 to move away from a focus on what the Sky leader ought to do in the mountains to what he could do. It was a rapid move to something which most stage racers take time to learn; you ride to your limit, then stay at your limit, rather than going over the edge. Because this is British Cycling, it was evidence-based: a calculation of how Wiggins would have fared in the 2010 Tour which showed he could have finished 11th rather than 23rd if he had raced within his limits. It's something that the greats – Hinault, LeMond, Indurain – could do instinctively, or with the help of a great *directeur sportif*. With Wiggins a relative novice and with no Cyrille Guimard figure to hand, Sky had to break it down and learn it.

■ Competition. Wiggins is legendary as a character who performs when his back is against the wall. He won't admit to it, but it is possible to speculate that his great 2012 stemmed in part from the arrival of Mark Cavendish at Sky late in 2011. Cavendish is known as a leader who rallies the group around him – the opposite of the relatively shy Wiggins, who agonises about how and when to thank his troops and has a tendency to go AWOL – and his impact was noted from the first training camp. It's also a fact that Cavendish represented competition, for all their close relationship, and Wiggins had to respond.

There were two chinks in Wiggins's armour: the first was his mental fragility. When he comes under assault unexpectedly, his first response is flight rather than fight, and it then falls to those around him to dust him down and keep him in the saddle. He's always been this way. Studying interviews we had done in 2004 and 2006, I was surprised to find that faced with the Millar and Floyd Landis scandals, his initial response was that he wanted to escape. Similarly, that was his first thought when Froome went, briefly, on the attack at La Toussuire. Not so much because he thought Froome was out to undermine him but because Wiggins craves certainty.

One of the core British Cycling principles is

controlling the things that can be controlled. Wiggins is the programme's ultimate pupil in his need for certainty. Hence his dislike of racing the first week of the Tour, that mayhem of crashes and injury which falls into a category of its own: a factor which can't be controlled but which can be influenced by judicious decision-making. Here, clearly, Sky were fluctuating between 'dithering', as Wiggins calls it – letting events happen in front of them – and taking control. They rode their luck, but made it at the same time, with Wiggins missing both the definitive pile-ups – at Boulogne and Metz – by a slender margin.

* * *

There is another factor beside sheer hard work and some breakthroughs on the coaching front that must have contributed to Wiggins winning the Tour. The creation of a more level playing field with improved drug testing and the UCI's recent ban on needles has favoured the Briton, who is adamant that he will never use drugs and has had no injections besides his vaccinations. Compare and contrast with the tales from the professional peloton of riders sitting on team buses post 2011, trying to get their heads around the fact that they have just been told that they are no longer allowed to use drips for recovery.

Wiggins comes out of a no-needle, no-drip culture at British Cycling. I would suggest that if the peloton is coming to terms with life without needles and drips for recovery using legal means – before we even start to think about illicit methods – a cyclist who has the background that Wiggins does will have a head start, as he highlighted back in 2011. His run of success began not long after the UCI brought in its needle ban; perhaps it's no coincidence.

'His strike rate this year is incredible and that's a good sign,' says Rob Hayles. Wiggins's former coaches Simon Jones and Matt Parker both recall how they would puzzle with him at time trials where their charge's power output would suggest he should have won. Wiggins himself wondered at times what the likes of Vinokourov were playing at – as he told *The Observer* at the 2007 Tour after 'Vino' smashed him in the Albi time trial. Then the Kazakh tested positive, and Wiggins wondered no longer.

There is another thesis that perhaps should do the rounds. I was told the tale of a former grand tour winner who felt he had no option but to seek time trialling advice in Britain. It seems his sheer lack of expertise in the area – aerodynamics, power transmission, testing, position on the tri-bars – was shocking. It was also intriguing that our rider and his team were subsequently unable to make good use of the expertise they sought out in Britain. They couldn't get the bikes built on time; they simply couldn't put into effect what they were advised to do.

Cycling's EPO and blood-doping culture goes

back 20 years. The priority for leading teams in the EPO years was blood enhancement; the supply of drugs and blood bags, and the concealment of their use from the dope testers and police. As Tyler Hamilton said in his book: you got your haematocrit up, and your weight down. That was most of what you needed. Given the ever-more elaborate and expensive methods of blood doping, technical expertise was replaced by reliance on doctors and soigneurs.

The experience of the grand tour winner and his time trial coach is not an isolated instance. In this year's Tour, one contender's supposed area of expertise was the descents, but that rider didn't go and reconnoitre those very downhills where he would have been expected to attack. Other contenders don't go and look at the time trials. All that leads me to believe that within professional cycling there is a 'technology gap', which the British, having explored every legal area of performance in the last 15 years, are perfectly placed to fill.

For years, British cyclists such as David Millar and Wiggins with experience of both British Cycling and European teams have been saying that in technical terms – training methods, the ability to break down the sport into its constituent parts, aerodynamics – much of professional cycling has lagged behind the British. In the mid-1990s Chris Boardman's ability to build to a specific target, his capacity to train and his attention to detail briefly took the peloton by storm.

Historically champions and cultures have tended to emerge from left field to pull the professional road side of the sport forwards. Think Fausto Coppi in the late 1940s; Greg LeMond in the 1980s; Francesco Moser (blood doping or no blood doping) earlier in the decade; infinitely more controversially, Lance Armstrong in the noughties – not in the sense of his doping, although he brought the leaders of the pack with him in that area, but in terms of global media profile. Less controversially, the Australians and the mountain bikers such as Cadel Evans and Ryder Hesjedal have emerged in recent years.

I would argue that the British cycling pyramid tipped by Team Sky but extending downwards through the track side of the sport in the UK is just the latest addition to that list. The sport's insiders have usually been surprised at the ease with which radical change occurs when it happens, but that should not be a shock: professional road cycling is a short-termist milieu, in which few sponsors invest for more than a few years.

National federations are strapped for cash. There are only rare instances of long-term, sustained investment such as that made by Sky since 2008, by Rabobank in Holland, until their shock departure in October 2012, and earlier by Mapei in the 1990s. There was such surprise at British Cycling's success in 2012 on road and track, but given 15 years of financial input from the Lottery and later from Sky, there should be no shock at all. If nothing had come of all that cash and expertise, now that would have been shocking.

My favourite story from Wiggins's book, *My Time*, is when he flies into Liège airport for the start of the 2012 Tour. It's the ultimate example of the marginal gains approach: he invests in a private jet – at his own expense – to minimise travelling time and exposure to possible infection from others. He lands in Liège to find Cadel Evans has flown in from the other direction, but with a big difference: no one has turned up to meet the 2011 Tour winner, although their hotel is close to the airport. If BMC can't even get that detail right, it's hardly surprising they didn't win the Tour.

David Millar sums up Wiggins perfectly: 'A very dedicated, driven, self-obsessed and ultimately sensible man... his ability to nail objectives is remarkable and comes from years of controlling variables and targeting one-off events on the track.' Given what Wiggins, Kerrison and Sutton put into 2012, the number of areas where they managed to move forwards and make marginal gains, it would have almost been surprising if he had not won the Tour.

William Fotheringham is the cycling correspondent for *The Guardian*. He ghost-wrote Bradley Wiggins's columns for both *The Guardian* and *Observer* from 2004 to 2012, and was the co-writer of Wiggins's account of his Tour de France and Olympic victories: *My Time*.

2

Thomas Voeckler is a rider who divides opinion.

As marginal gains accelerate the march towards cycling by numbers, Voeckler stands out as a rough diamond to cherish – an emotionally-engaging underdog without whom professional racing would be a lot duller.

Edward Pickering writes in defence of modern cycling's greatest attacking force.

IN PRAISE OF THOMAS VOECKLER

BY EDWARD PICKERING

Tell me what you think about Thomas Voeckler and I'll tell you what your world view is.

I remember having an argument with a friend once about tennis. Pete Sampras was about to play Andre Agassi in the Wimbledon final, and my friend was fully behind Sampras, while I wanted Agassi to win. What my friend admired about Sampras – his elegant, languid class and effortless style – was precisely what made me want his opponent to win.

Aesthetically, Sampras was perfect. Too perfect. I wanted the underdog – the scurrying, imperfect, punchy, emotional Agassi – to prevail. I didn't want a masterclass in efficient match-winning. I wanted to be emotionally engaged, to feel like Agassi could somehow overturn the inevitability of defeat against a better player through willpower alone.

Of course, Sampras won.

Thomas Voeckler is a bit like Agassi: living proof that wanting to win goes a long way towards not losing. Put him up against Bradley Wiggins in the Tour de France, and there's no competition – class beats aggression every time over the three weeks of a grand tour (especially when helped along by stifling tactics and domestiques who could be leaders in most other teams). But put Voeckler in a break, in whatever terrain, and he'll turn himself inside out to put his front wheel over the line first.

'Je me suis sorti des tripes,' Voeckler often says after a race. If you want to beat him, you've got to be ready to ride hard enough that you puke up your internal organs, too. Voeckler, according to his team manager Jean-René Bernaudeau, is also a 'computer' – his tactical brain is quick, and his racing decisions are usually right.

There are few other cyclists who genuinely put me on the edge of my seat when I'm watching bike races. Voeckler's riding is visceral, and it provokes a physical reaction in me. As he bent his back with the effort of winning the 10th stage of this year's Tour de France, a desperate slow-motion uphill grind to the finish in Bellegarde-sur-Valserine, I recall subconsciously twisting in my chair, willing him to win.

His racing style is compelling, human. But it's not to everybody's taste. One of his nicknames is 'Hollywood', because what some perceive as plucky aggression, others perceive as ego. He's not universally popular with other riders, for the same reasons.

But to describe him as either doughty fighter, tactical genius or egotistical show-off is to miss the point. Voeckler holds a mirror up to cycling fans, reflecting their own prejudices and desires for the sport.

Cycling fans exist along a spectrum. At one end, you have subjective fans; at the other, objective.

Subjective fans get a kick from the emotional attachment of picking a favourite rider or team, and supporting them whatever happens. When they win, there is a boost in self-esteem. When they lose, the fans suffer disappointment. A lot of football fans are towards the subjective end of the spectrum, and some would argue that the England rugby team forces their supporters to be subjective – to support the England rugby team is to acknowledge that winning ugly beats losing pretty. But the emotional attachment overrides aesthetic concerns.

For objective fans, sport is the thing. Who cares who wins, as long as the battle is entertaining and the narrative compelling? In cycling, in anglophone countries especially, with few home favourites to cheer, the fandom used to tend towards the objective (although Lance Armstrong brought in a lot of North American fans who paid attention to only one thing – their man winning, and, judging by this summer, Team Sky and Bradley Wiggins may well do the same in the UK).

Of course, there are many other motivations for being a fan but, at base level, subjective fans like to see their rider win, while objective fans like to see the riders race.

The funny thing about Thomas Voeckler is that

he seems to sit right in the middle of the subjective/objective spectrum. His character means that fans can easily connect emotionally to his racing, making him popular with subjective fans. But his do-or-die attacking and tactical nous makes him attractive to objective fans.

You might think it would make him universally popular, but all it seems to do is accentuate the differences between the fans.

* * *

The 2012 Tour felt like a watershed in tactics and style. There was a paradigm shift in the way Bradley Wiggins won the yellow jersey – the fact that the Brit rode the same way, with the same result, in Paris-Nice, the Tour of Romandy, the Critérium du Dauphiné and the Tour de France, made it seem like cycling had changed on a profound level. The Tour, that anarchic, three-week-long festival of unpredictability and daily upheaval, had finally been conquered by science, discipline and logic.

Wiggins and his team had worked out that if they could ride at a certain number of watts for a certain number of minutes, nobody would be able to attack in the mountains, and he could then clean up in the time trials. This is not to say that it was easy – physically, it's as hard as cycling can be, and Wiggins still had to ride faster than everybody else.

Voeckler was the antidote to Team Sky's control. His role in the 2012 Tour was, along with a few privileged others, to provide the excitement. If the battle for the general classification was being won by science, Voeckler was fighting a rearguard action for art. He got into breaks, frowned, shouted at his rivals, gurned, rocked all over his bike, stuck his tongue out, and took two stages and the king of the mountains jersey.

The public loved it and, on one hand, so did I. Voeckler races how I like to think I would, if only I had stronger legs and better resistance to pain.

When he fought his way up the Col de Peyresourde en route to his second stage win in Luchon, through a parting sea of baying spectators, I fancied that more young fans would imagine themselves as him, riding solo to a heroic win, than they would as Bradley Wiggins, tapping up in a protective cocoon of team-mates.

I waited for Voeckler on the finish line in Luchon, at the bottom of the Peyresourde, on a kiln-hot day – the hottest of the Tour – where riders would come in crusted in salt, dried spit, blood and roadburn, and the boisterous reaction of the crowd reflected Voeckler's popularity.

If the fans had seen what I had, at the back of the presentation podium before he received the plaudits of the crowd – Voeckler collapsing to the floor and having to sit down for a few minutes while he recovered from his efforts – they'd have liked him even more. Later on, I waited at the team bus as Jean-René Bernaudeau welcomed back his riders, one by one, in the middle of an enraptured crush of hundreds of fans, far more than for any other team – even Sky. Voeckler's a once-in-a-generation sporting hero, a Poulidor or Virenque for the 21st century.

But, on the other hand, the more Voeckler plays the role of sporting hero, the more cemented the stereotype becomes in the minds of the public. And I've learned over the years that there is a considerable distance between Voeckler the sporting hero and Voeckler the person. He may bludgeon his way through bike races with his tongue hanging out and his doughy face moulded into a grimace, but that's not how he goes through life. What's he really like?

* * *

I first interviewed Voeckler in 2005, and I've spent the subsequent seven-and-a-half years trying to work out what makes him tick. I'm not sure I'm any closer to knowing now than I was at the start, but I've spent enough time watching him to know that he is both protected, and done a disservice, by the mythology that has sprung up around him.

It goes back to the 2004 Tour, when he surfed a cresting wave of circumstances and momentum to take and hold the yellow jersey for 10 days. The

French loved his spirited defence of the race lead and, though it was five years before he really shone at the Tour again (with a stage win in 2009), and seven before he reprised his original spell in yellow with another one, even more tenaciously-defended, his popularity never seemed to waver.

Other riders, notably Sylvain Chavanel, achieved better results between 2004 and 2011. But Chavanel never matched Voeckler's popularity – there was something about Voeckler that resonated.

It was a combination of many things – a dramatic and attacking racing style, a down-to-earth confidence, the perception that he wore his heart on his sleeve, a pleasant face and a nice smile. He's not classically good-looking, but his boyish looks seem to bring out a protective instinct in fans, especially female ones.

Voeckler often races without sunglasses, or with clear lenses. Whether this is deliberate, I don't know, but it makes him more accessible. When Voeckler races, I feel like I have eye contact with him, while other riders hide themselves behind dark lenses.

Commentators and the media latched on to all these things, and Voeckler's cycling persona, his myth, started feeding off itself in a reinforcing spiral.

On one hand, Thomas Voeckler the sporting personality doesn't really exist – he is a construct which is lazily reinforced by the clichés and assumptions of the fans and media. On the other hand, this construct handily protects Voeckler from the excesses of celebrity.

When he's not on the front page of *L'Equipe*, or filling the screens during a televisual attack on the Tour de France, there's not much of the celebrity about Voeckler, however.

I spent a few days at the Europcar team's training camp in Alicante in January 2012 to interview Voeckler for *Cycle Sport* magazine, but also to watch him and his team-mates away from the races, where tiredness, transfers and pressure cause riders to withdraw into their shells.

Voeckler may inspire the same passion as Richard Virenque did in the 1990s and early 2000s (although without the same complex relationship with doping products), but there's no similarity in how they treat their celebrity. Virenque always carried his celebrity self-consciously. He wore designer clothes and embraced his role as housewives' favourite enthusiastically. Voeckler, on the other hand, doesn't.

My first sighting of him in Alicante came when he was running late for a webchat organised by his team. Whoever was hosting it was obviously a gambling man, because they'd written, 'Thomas is now here to answer your questions' just as somebody came running through the lobby asking, 'Where's Thomas?'

A few minutes later he came shambling through in his team tracksuit, looking like he'd just woken up.

Voeckler wasn't in great shape at the camp, though one of the team managers confided to me that none of the riders were, and that it was a cause for concern. He was still strong enough to lead his team-mates up the climbs on the group rides, huffing and puffing, his face flushing pink with the effort, but it was hard to believe this was the rider who'd come fourth at the Tour de France just six months previously.

Though he was sociable with his team-mates and sat with them in the bar during the evenings, when the raucous laughter that is always the soundtrack to gatherings of young men echoed through the hotel, he generally gave the impression of somebody who didn't really want to be there.

The reasons for this became clear when we did our interview, when he talked a lot about trying to live a normal life away from cycling. First, when he's not racing, he's a committed house-husband. He does the school run and the housework in between training rides – 'I'm not too important to push a vacuum cleaner round the house,' he laughed. His kids routinely appear at the Tour on rest days – he did his press conference at Pau last year, alongside La Toussuire stage winner Pierre Rolland, with a toddler bouncing on his lap.

Secondly, he doesn't enjoy training.

To understand the way Voeckler races, you have to understand that competition, and winning, is what motivates him to cycle. He's not one to enjoy a pleasant five-hour ride in the countryside and he's not in cycling to look at the scenery. He loves competing and he loves beating people, and he's prepared to hurt himself quite seriously to do so.

Pain is the constant companion of the professional cyclist. All tolerate it. Some even enjoy it. But Voeckler is one of a few who seem to wallow in it. On that Tour stage victory in Bellegarde, the leading group changed from a coherent unit of five riders into a pub brawl on the run-in to the finish. Voeckler was all over his bike for the final kilometre, and couldn't even raise his hands in victory as he crossed the line.

He'd beaten Michele Scarponi, Jens Voigt, Luis Leon Sanchez and Dries Devenyns, yet the only thing I could be sure of as the riders approached Bellegarde was that any one of them could have won. To say that Voeckler won because he fought harder and dug deeper than his rivals is to miss the point that Voeckler's timing and tactics were also superior to those of the others.

Devenyns made a serious attack with two kilometres to go and gained a lot of ground, but was chased down. When Voeckler went, he was pursued for a long time by Luis Leon Sanchez, but the Spaniard could only hold the gap, not close it – they were more or less equal in strength, but Voeckler's timing had been better. Then Jens Voigt and Michele

Scarponi chased, and they looked faster than Voeckler, but Scarponi could only close to three seconds at the line. All five looked wasted at the finish, all five could legitimately say they had '*s'est sorti des tripes*', but only Voeckler had combined grit with correct tactics. So much for plucky Thomas Voeckler – he'd had the coolest head of all of them.

Or maybe he did want it more. Voeckler's backstory includes the terrible tragedy of his father, missing at sea, presumed dead. When you have endured something like that, the physical pain of bike racing may be easier to tolerate. But this is something we can never know, although it suits us to build it into Voeckler's narrative.

The Frenchman is a lightning rod for opinions among cycling fans. He seems to inspire adoration and contempt in equal measure, generally because of how we have built up his mythology.

I've spent a lot of time trying to work out what makes Thomas Voeckler tick, but I've realised that the interesting thing about him is that ability of his to hold up a mirror to cycling fans and the media.

Whatever you think about him, it says as much about you as it does him.

Edward Pickering is better at cycling than most writers, and better at writing than most cyclists. This combination of skills made a career in cycling journalism the obvious choice. He is the deputy editor of *Cycle Sport*, and co-author with Robbie McEwen of *One Way Road*.

3

Rupert Guinness follows the long road from Australia's first Tour de France competitors in 1914 to the nation's first professional team to compete in the race almost a century on.

Winning might not always come easy to a team in its infancy but in 2012 Orica-GreenEdge have blazed quite a trail and will look to improve further in 2013.

Can they better their YouTube video though?

THE NEW WIZARDS OF OZ

BY RUPERT GUINNESS

When the Orica-GreenEdge team made their Tour de France debut in 2012, they readily revealed their intention: to win a stage and compete for – if not win – the green points jersey. By the time the 3,497-kilometre Tour had finished, however, both objectives remained unfulfilled.

Before the start of the race, the Australian team's general manager, Shayne Bannan, stated: 'It would be good if we can win a stage or two. If we can at least show people that we can be competitive... To not be placed in stages would be disappointing.'

To that end, the team ticked the box: Matt Goss – the squad's big hope for a stage win and the green jersey – took second place three times and added another handful of top 10 places.

He was also relegated from sixth to seventh on stage 12 for his illegal sprint against Peter Sagan of Liquigas, which cost him 30 points in the race for the green jersey.

Goss's Swiss team-mate, Michael Albasini, clinched his best result – fifth – on stage three, after appearing in several breaks, while South African Daryl Impey took fifth place on stage 13.

But considering their lofty ambitions and early-season successes, their debut Tour could be deemed a disappointment, especially when you consider that their pre-race hopes, Simon Gerrans and Dutchman Pieter Weening, failed to fire in the hillier stages.

What the results really highlight is not so much any major failing, but the difficulties a new team – both the riders and staff – faces when trying to gel at an optimal level for the world's biggest race, where every rival is at his peak and riders and teams are exposed for the slightest of their vulnerabilities.

Looking back at Orica-GreenEdge's Tour debut, it's hard to criticise what in its basic form was such a significant chapter of Australian cycling history without sounding like the Grinch ruining Christmas. Australian cycling fans could be rightly proud of the first Australian team to take part in the Tour.

It had been an unfulfilled dream for many years. The seed was planted in 1914 when Don Kirkham and Snowy Munro became the first two Australians to ride the Tour. And the dream grew as other Australian riders followed the daring duo in the years that followed. They included the celebrated Sir Hubert Opperman, Ernie Bainbridge and Percy Osborne, who raced the Tour in 1928, then Frankie Thomas, Richard 'Fatty' Lamb and Ossie Nicholson, teaming up with Opperman in 1931. John Beasley followed in 1952 and 1955, Russell Mockridge in 1953, Bill Lawrie in 1967 and Don Allan in 1974 and 1975 before Phil Anderson really blazed a trail.

Anderson was the first Australian to wear the race leader's jersey in 1981, before going on to place in the top 10 overall five times, including two fifth place finishes, during a 14-year career.

After Anderson, a stream of Aussies forged careers in Europe as 'super domestiques', stage winners, points and overall classification contenders, culminating in Robbie McEwen winning the first of his green jerseys in 2002 and Cadel Evans claiming the ultimate prize – overall Tour de France victory – in 2011.

When GreenEdge said in 2011 that it would become the latest party to try to start an Australian team, it was seen as a natural progression.

But while Orica-GreenEdge said all along they would not have a rider vying for the overall classification, they knew there was pressure to get results – for their main sponsor, the mining explosives giant Orica, which signed for three years just before the 2012 Giro d'Italia, for Australian cycling and for their fans.

And despite a successful start to their first season – matched by a similar sparkle at the back end of the year – there was some disappointment following a Tour without a stage win. Their biggest flaw appeared to be that they placed so much early emphasis on trying to win the green jersey rather than get a stage win.

When McEwen won his three green jerseys in 2002, 2004 and 2006, he always made claiming that first stage win his first priority. It's easy to see why he did. After Goss lost his 30 points on stage 12, he and the team just didn't have the energy left to pull off the stage win they so wanted. They were spent from chasing points and watching Sagan dance round them.

It was also clear that Orica-GreenEdge had underestimated the potential of the Slovakian Sagan. Earlier in the season, at the three-week Giro d'Italia, head sports director Matt White declared that the Tour's battle for the green jersey would be a two-rider race between Goss and defending champion Mark Cavendish of Sky. White's confidence was buoyed by Orica-GreenEdge's showing at the Giro where a potentially formidable sprint train emerged.

Orica-GreenEdge will no doubt continue to work on perfecting that train, which is primarily focused on getting Goss, the 2011 World Championship silver medallist behind Briton Cavendish, across the line first. And the commitment to that goal is totally justified.

Goss, also the 2011 Milan-San Remo winner, is an exceptional sprinter. Cavendish has repeatedly said of all the sprinters in the peloton, his former team-mate is the one he fears most.

The Australian team may be one reputed for sniffing out winning chances. They are openly opportunists. But the team is also heavily focused on trying to clinch wins in bunch sprints, even if it became clear by the end of their first year that they still have some way to go to hone their sprint train's strength.

It helped that at the Giro, in the 190-kilometre third stage out and back from Horsens, in Denmark, Orica-GreenEdge nabbed their first grand tour stage win with Goss.

However, while its value was perhaps lessened by Cavendish crashing with 125 metres to go, what many did not know was that the Australian team had put into practice a plan aimed at beating Cavendish that, at the time of his crash, looked to be working perfectly.

The self-belief that they could beat Cavendish counted for a lot: many teams go into a sprint thinking that if Cavendish is there he can't be beaten. But not Orica-GreenEdge, as I discovered on the team meeting in their bus that day as White outlined the blueprint for their 'mission impossible' – so called due to Cavendish's speed and the sheer strength of his British Sky team.

Standing in the back room of the $450,000 custom-made bus, White's calm three-and-a-half minute address impressed.

He empathised with Goss for the weight of

frustration on him, having succumbed to five second places in his previous eight races.

But White also knew that for Goss to break the run – especially against Cavendish – it was imperative that his pep talk focused not on the negatives of the previous day, but on the positives.

First up for White on the last of the Giro's three days in Denmark, as he addressed his eclectic mix of riders, hailing from Australia, Slovenia, Japan, Belgium, South Africa and Canada, was to revisit the previous day's racing in stage two in Herning, where Goss was second by a bike's length.

'It was a good ride by Gossy,' White told his riders in the meeting. 'He gave it every chance yesterday. In the finale... it was a very hectic sprint. I was happy with [having] guys up there. It wasn't as co-ordinated as we would have liked. No teams really nailed that finish yesterday. But the pleasing thing is that you guys have got legs, you've got balls to get in there and have a go. But today, on a much tighter circuit, we want to really nail the finish, especially from the two-kilometres-to-go mark.'

Then came cycling's 'C' word: Cavendish.

'We know that, with Cavendish, we can count the times on one hand that he has had to come over other riders,' White said. 'In all his sprints, he is the first guy when he starts the sprint. There are only a couple of sprints he has ever done where he has been passed. So, for us to beat Cavendish, we have got to deliver Gossy in front of Mark. Nine times out of 10, Cav is going to beat Gossy if Gossy starts from behind.

'That's the best way,' White continued, 'the only way, really, to beat him. He has shown he is the fastest guy in the world, so we have to force Sky to make mistakes, or we have to nail it better.

'To do that, we can't get caught out on a tight circuit with two kilometres to go. We want to deliver our train to that corner, then the last four guys can take care of the rest.'

White went on to talk about the final lead-out for Goss by South Africa's Daryl Impey, Lithuanian Tomas Vaitkus, and Australian Brett Lancaster, and the all-important need for patience, especially from the less experienced riders such as Jack Bobridge, who was taking part in his first road race since the track World Championships track a month earlier.

'Like yesterday, if there is any chasing that needs to be done, Christian [Meier] will do the chasing. But everyone else... just look after yourself,' White said.

'Jack, you just stay in the bunch – we don't want to see you all day until we get to the [finishing] circuits. Then, we all have to hit the circuits very far in front. We want to be the first team with numbers into that tight corner. All right?'

White's riders didn't say a word. Their answer came hours later with the sight of them, strength in numbers at the front, with Goss over the line first.

Still, the Orica-GreenEdge sprint train remains a work in progress. The Lotto-Belisol squad, working for the German powerhouse André Greipel, has taken time to be as strong as it is.

Despite the Giro stage win, White's opinion that the Tour green jersey battle would be between Cavendish and Goss, and not Sagan, surprised many considering Sagan had won five stages at the Tour of California in May. White cited Sagan's age (then 22), inexperience and suspect ability to last three weeks.

By the end of the Tour, White conceded that Sagan had proved him wrong, although in mitigation it could be said that the race for the green jersey was not a conventional scrap between the sprinters.

* * *

Orica-GreenEdge should arrive at the 2013 Tour older and wiser. When all was said and done, their 2012 season was a resounding success, with 31 victories by October – the latest being Svein Tuft and Luke Durbridge's win at the Duo Normand two-man time trial in northern France.

It was a haul that a number of more established teams would have happily ended the season with.

Besides Goss's Giro stage win, those victories included wins by Gerrans in the Australian road race championships, the Tour Down Under, Milan-San Remo and the Grand Prix de Quebec; Albasini with two stages and the overall classification at the Volta a Catalunya in Spain and a stage at the Tour of Switzerland; wins for Impey at the Tour of the Basque Country and Tour of Slovenia; a stage and the overall for Australian Luke Durbridge at the Circuit de la Sarthe, victory in the prologue of the Critérium du Dauphiné, as well as a stage and overall honours in the Tour du Poitou Charentes, and with it the best young rider's jersey.

At the same race, Lithuanian Aidis Kruopis also won a stage and the points jersey competition, as well as a stage of the Tour of Poland, and then Australian Simon Clarke took a stage and the king of the mountains title at the Vuelta a España.

There was also success for the women's team, which raced as Orica-AIS under sport directors Martin Barras and former pro Dave McPartland. Their season included domination of the Bay Criteriums series, the national titles and the Tour of Oman, a string of top results in Classics and stage races, and a silver medal in the trade team time trial at the World Championships in the Netherlands where a retiring Judith Arndt also won the individual time trial.

***

Following the team's inaugural season, some concerns have emerged, even if they've not been openly spoken of. It was not lost on some observers that the squad's main sponsor, Orica, has a track record of controversy.

GreenEdge, the team's management company, promoted am environmental image in its infancy, but that image appeared challenged when Orica was named as a headline sponsor shortly before the Giro. GreenEdge countered the critics by saying that the sponsorship was a commitment by Orica to work on its environmental standing. But in September, nearing the season's end, the mining explosives company was prosecuted for the fifth time in 2012 after breaching a pollution licence at its plant in Botany, Sydney.

The Environmental Protection Agency said it was related to the emission of mercury vapour near a residential area in September 2011.

Of course, that was outside of the cycling team's control, but even before the season had ended, the seeds of several considerable concerns began to emerge. First up was the loss of one of up-and-coming star Jack Bobridge to Dutch team Rabobank, even though he had a year left on his contract.

Bobridge, a key member of Australia's 2012 Olympic Games silver-medal team pursuit line-up, and the reigning world record holder over 4,000 metres, had long been touted as a star in the making, blessed as he is with an incredible engine.

However, soon after the Giro d'Italia, where a foot injury had forced him to abandon with a day to go, the South Australian ran foul of the law in

Spain, where he lives in Girona, for a drink driving incident at Lloret de Mar, also involving Australian squad team-mate and soon-to-be Orica-GreenEdge recruit Michael Hepburn.

Bobridge later made a 'full disclosure' to the Australian Olympic team *chef de mission* Nick Green that saved his selection for the London Olympics. But in the Spanish courts he was fined and lost his licence for eight months. Cycling Australia also put him on a 12-month good behaviour bond, fined him $2,500, and put an indefinite drinking ban on him for whenever he's on the national team. Hepburn, meanwhile, was placed on a 12-month good behaviour bond and fined $1,000.

Orica-GreenEdge, too, was understood to have placed severe restrictions on Bobridge that were not to his liking, leading to his exit. That Bobridge's move to Rabobank was granted by Orica-GreenEdge indicated that the feeling was mutual.

Another concern that one can only hope remains as such and does not prove to be problematic is the effectiveness of the leadership pathway in place for the team's current and up-and-coming stars with such an abundance of former Australian riders in management and staff positions.

Neil Stephens is an experienced former professionals from a good generation or two before most of the team's riders. But with strong characters like Robbie McEwen and Matt Wilson, who began the team's first year as riders but have since retired to take staff positions, and with whispers of the evergreen Stuart O'Grady destined to be offered a director's role, Orica-GreenEdge may find their young riders suffocated by the strong minds of those recently retired riders now in consultancy or sports director roles, and unable to naturally develop their leadership skills through trial and error.

* * *

By the time the 2012 Tour de France got under way in Liège, the journey travelled had been a lot more successful than Orica-GreenEdge general manager Shayne Bannan had expected when presented with the opportunity to set up Australia's first top-tier team back in July 2010.

Bannan, then Cycling Australia's high performance director, was behind the wheel of his car on an Italian *autostrada*, driving a group of Australian junior riders to a race in Bergamo, when his mobile phone rang.

It was Gerry Ryan – a Melbourne businessman who owns the Jayco caravan company with his son Andrew, and whose wealth in 2010 was estimated at $180 million. Ryan is also the majority owner of Global Creatures, the production company behind the animatronics arena production *Walking With Dinosaurs*, which grossed more than $350 million worldwide between its 2007 launch and 2010.

A long-time supporter of Australian cycling, having sponsored Cycling Australia, the Victorian Institute of Sport and a number of races, Ryan has become a public figure within Australian sport – especially in Melbourne.

In recent years, he has also sponsored the Melbourne Storm National Rugby League team, the St Kilda AFL club, cricket, horse racing, basketball and lawn bowls.

Bannan readily recalled Ryan's call on that July day in 2010: 'He said, "I'd like to talk to you about something. Can you come to Paris?"'

Ryan was in France, following the Tour in the Pyrenees, three days away from the finish on the Champs-Élysées in the French capital.

The call and invitation from Ryan to meet in Paris – brief and short of detail though it was – concerned Bannan at first.

'I was worried that Gerry was going to withdraw his funding from the national programme,' Bannan said. 'I hung up, and then started wondering, what are we going to do now?'

Fortunately for Bannan – and the young Australian cyclists in his car, and others like them whose futures he feared were on the line – Ryan called back and said: 'Shayne, I should have been more specific. I'm still at the Tour and I'm wondering how we can get an Australian team here.'

In that moment, the seed was planted in Bannan's mind for a plan that would rapidly grow into what first became known as the GreenEdge project and then developed into the Orica-GreenEdge team making its historic Tour debut in 2012.

To say Bannan was relieved Ryan spoke nothing of pulling funds from the national programme would be an understatement. But that Ryan spoke of creating a UCI WorldTour team that would need 30 riders, 37 staff and be ranked in the top 18 in the world to make the 2012 Tour, requiring an estimated annual budget of $10-12 million to keep it going, according to UCI licensing laws, left Bannan 'shaking like a leaf in excitement', he said.

'But I knew straight away that with that dream comes a lot of processes, and that there was a heap of work to be done,' said Bannan, who had long dreamed of setting up an Australian pro team.

As Bannan drove on, with the Australian junior riders in his car chatting among themselves, the 'must do' list began mounting. After dropping the riders off for their race, Bannan continued driving to Brescia, where he met up with Neil Stephens, who was Cycling Australia's professional co-ordinator, and was working with another pro team at the time.

Stephens would join Bannan on the GreenEdge project, and the two men worked on a rough blueprint to put to Ryan in Paris two days later.

On a balmy Saturday afternoon – the day

before the 2010 Tour finished on the Champs-Élysées, where Spaniard Alberto Contador claimed a third win that he would later lose for doping – Bannan sat with Ryan at a small café in the Opera district. He presented his blueprint to Ryan, who in turn expanded on his reasons for wanting to support it and revealed that his vision was not confined to a men's team, but a top women's team, too.

* * *

On Sunday, January 16, 2011, several hours before the Cancer Council Classic criterium in Adelaide – two days before the Tour Down Under – the GreenEdge project was officially launched by Bannan.

By December that year, GreenEdge had morphed into a real top-tier team, awarded with one of 18 prized UCI licences, allowing it to race in all World-Tour events, including the grand tours of Italy, France and Spain.

And Bannan said that the person to thank the most was Ryan who guaranteed the estimated $20 million start costs and $10-12 million annual budget to the end of 2013.

'With Gerry and the Ryan family, it has not been a two-minute involvement... They've been involved for years. He is a man with vision,' he said.

The creation of the team was far from straight-forward, though. Almost as soon as the GreenEdge

project had been launched, Bannan and Stephens
set about planning and secretly recruiting riders
and staff – despite the UCI's controversial deadline
which means that riders are unable to negotiate with
potential new employers until August 1, officially at
least.

Possible locations were also scouted out for the
team's service course – a headquarters in which to
house the squad's equipment – while cars, trucks and
buses were also required.

However, with Ryan's backing for three years
guaranteed, there was no rush to sign a principal
sponsor. The thinking was that the team could start
as GreenEdge, allowing the squad time to raise its
value with results, and in the meantime promote
its brand. 'Green' signified the green of Australia's
green and gold colours, as well as an environmentally
friendly touch. 'Edge' reinforced the constant search
for a winning advantage.

'We don't even know what our product is worth
now,' Bannan said at the time. 'If we under-sell now,
we will be locked in for two to three years.'

The priority for GreenEdge was to secure sponsors for equipment and vehicles. First to confirm that
they were on board were Scott bikes, Santini clothing
and Subaru cars, while other potential suppliers were
courted at the Eurobike trade show in Germany in
August 2011.

The overriding aim was for the GreenEdge name

to be promoted nationwide, and to become as keenly supported in Australia as other national teams like the Wallabies rugby union side.

Signing riders was a must, yet not so easy for a new team – nor cheap.

GreenEdge initially aimed at a 28-rider roster, but ended up recruiting the maximum allowed of 30 with 75 per cent being Australian. Between them, the signed riders had enough world ranking points to secure their UCI ProTeam licence.

GreenEdge made no secret of their plans not to sign a grand tour contender, which would have set them back somewhere between $1.4 million a year to the estimated $5.5 million that a Tour de France winner might command.

Instead, they targeted young Australian prospects like Cameron Meyer, then 23, and Jack Bobridge, 22, as well as proven stage and Classic winners such as Australians Simon Gerrans and Stuart O'Grady, and Dutchmen Pieter Weening and Sebastian Langeveld.

While Bannan knew general classification riders would not come cheap, he cited state-of-the-art facilities such as the Australian Institute of Sport's European Training Centre in Varese, in northern Italy, which was opened in March 2011, as a lure to the riders he was targeting.

The ETC was a unique element GreenEdge could offer potential recruits that other teams could not, having come to a commercial arrangement with the

centre to have its administrative and athletes' headquarters there, allowing its riders access to all training, rehabilitation and sport science facilities.

Accommodation and full restaurant services are
also available for riders visiting for medical attention,
or to undergo rehabilitation programmes, to meet
GreenEdge management for consultation on training and racing programmes, or contract negotiations.
It is also a team base for training camps for riders not
racing at any one period during the season.

The team's service course ended up being a 2,200
square metre building in Brunello, about a kilometre-
and-a-half from the Cycling Australia national team
base at nearby Castronno, where the Australian men's
under-23 Jayco-AIS and national women's teams are
based. Having everything so close together meant it
was like a little bit of Australia in Varese.

That November, GreenEdge were to learn if
they would get a ProTeam licence, and there was still
much to do to convince the UCI that they deserved
the golden ticket to the world's biggest races. The
next option for the Australian team would have been
to obtain a 'second division' ProContinental licence,
but that would have left their chances of racing in
the top races hinging on 'wildcard' invitations.

For a licence, teams must fulfil criteria in such
areas as sporting value (a team's roster), ethical policy
(anti-doping and code of conduct), financial viability
(sponsorship, marketing and business structure) and

development plans (men's under-23 and women's teams, talent identification).

Besides riders, GreenEdge also had to recruit staff, and by early 2011 Bannan was already receiving about 10 emails a day from all over the world – from soigneurs [masseurs], mechanics, sports directors, and even chefs wanting jobs, Bannan said.

He said that 85 per cent of applications for the full-time positions were from people already working for ProTeam squads, which offered the team vast experience straight away.

'If we started with too many novices, there would be the potential of not having enough experience for pressured situations,' he pointed out.

By August, 90 per cent of the staff positions had been filled.

Heading the line-up alongside director Andrew Ryan, Bannan, technical director Neil Stephens and chief medical and welfare director Peter Barnes would be Matt White as head sports director.

There would be two more sports directors, plus six to eight soigneurs, six to eight mechanics, two more doctors, two to three physiotherapists, two physiologists and office staff.

By November, everything was in place, and all that was needed was the UCI to anoint GreenEdge with ProTeam status.

That call came in December, in a year when interest in cycling in Australia soared after Cadel Evans's

Tour de France win. The Australian might have been contracted to the American BMC outfit, but Evans was openly a supporter of the GreenEdge project. Prior to the ProTeam licence announcement, Ryan remained quietly confident.

That calm was evident when I spoke with Ryan at a civic reception in Melbourne held for Evans after his Tour victory parade. The timing of Evans's Tour win in the pointy end of their 18-month campaign to get up and running was not lost on Ryan.

As for the lack of a main sponsor, it wasn't a concern for Ryan.

'It's about building the brand – the GreenEdge army,' he said. 'We want to appeal to Australians, but not only Australians... Since signing Pieter Weening, Dutch interest, in terms of hits on the team website, has been running at about 24 per cent. In Australia, the interest is only about 48 per cent. The rest of it is international.'

He felt the build-up to their wait for the UCI license was virtually trouble free. One hiccup that did not go unnoticed, however, was the sudden decision to let GreenEdge's first chief executive, Mike McKay, a former member of the 'Oarsome Foursome' coxless four Olympic rowing champions, go.

Melbourne-based McKay's tenure was short-lived, and it was clear during a GreenEdge public relations trip to the Giro d'Italia that year, attended by journalists – including me – that there was a difference in philosophy between McKay and the GreenEdge management structure in place.

Ryan would not elaborate on McKay's departure that came soon after the Giro, other than to say that the Australian-based position would not be filled.

'It's forgotten, to be honest,' Ryan said. 'There hasn't been any change. It never had any impact on GreenEdge, and the role of CEO won't be replaced. Pending the sponsor, we are going to put the right people in to deliver the requirements of the sponsor. A manager rather than a CEO.'

Ryan also revealed an insight into what he was expecting from GreenEdge in its first year, and in the seasons to follow, from the young riders signed.

Asked, as a businessman, what would determine whether GreenEdge's first season would be deemed a success, Ryan replied: 'It depends on your expectations. If you want to talk business-speak, it's in terms of your KPIs [key performance indicators]: to be accepted into the ProTeam circuit is our number one priority. Number two is to have developed the right culture and to be getting the right riders. We are not expecting to win a grand tour, although we would like to be in that position five years from now. If we have the right riders, we want to be competitive. We have gone after youth and are prepared to have patience to develop those kids and bring enough experience in so they have that leadership.

'For the younger guys, the [2012] Olympic Games

are the priority over riding the Tour or the Giro d'Italia,' he continued. 'Their programme will be based around the Olympic Games. They are stepping up and maturing and will be ready to go in 2013.'

Ryan's vision wasn't just focused on a men's team, either. As Bannan learned when he spoke with Ryan in Paris in July 2010, Ryan's conviction for women's cycling was just as deep rooted.

'We will have a women's team [run under] the same philosophy as the men's,' Ryan said firmly, adding: 'Women have been neglected. We want the women's team to be part of the scene as per Australian women's basketball, where a major sponsor is there to give women the opportunity to participate and grow by having that international competition.'

Ryan also saw a broader *raison d'etre* for the creation of the GreenEdge organisation.

'It's an opportunity for Australians on the team, and not just its riders. The management, doctors, physios and sports scientists will have a stepping stone to the world stage,' said Ryan. 'That's how we become better. In all my businesses, we benchmark ourselves off international companies. Australia is such a small market. You limit your thinking, your growth, by not being international.'

However, Ryan was less direct about his view on internal discipline – an area that was a key element in their application to the UCI for a ProTeam licence, other than to say: 'We have a strong code in place.

But we want to develop a strong culture and that culture comes from the top.'

When pressed as to whether a breach of that code – whether it concerned doping or any other form of ill-discipline – would mean him withdrawing his support for GreenEdge, Ryan replied: 'No... If an individual breaks it, why should one individual affect the rest of the team?'

This led to Ryan being asked if he was concerned about Neil Stephens, employed as technical director, having been implicated in the 1998 Festina doping scandal as a rider at the Tour, and Matt White, who then had yet to join GreenEdge but had been named in the investigation into the US Postal Service team he once rode for following doping allegations against Lance Armstrong, by Floyd Landis in 2010.

'No,' Ryan replied. 'Both of them have coached in Australia. Obviously the Australian Sports Commission and Cycling Australia have done their homework and research and have gone through the process.'

Had he spoken to them about it?

'No – never,' Ryan said.

* * *

The team debuted as GreenEdge at the Jayco Bay Cycling Classic Series in Victoria in January 2012. A few days later, Simon Gerrans won the Australian road race championship in a temporary team strip, helping to boost anticipation ahead of their World-Tour debut at the Tour Down Under in Adelaide in mid-January, where they unveiled their first official jersey. The team later unveiled another jersey at the Giro after Orica had signed as their sponsor, and then a revised fourth version at the Tour de France.

The team's debut didn't enjoy the fairytale start they had hoped for, however. Before a pedal had even been turned in anger, the team became embroiled in a controversy when O'Grady found his name and face in the media following a car chauffeur's allegations of drunken behaviour during the drive back to his home in Adelaide after a function.

While it soon became clear that there was conjecture about the veracity of the claims against O'Grady, for which no charges were laid, the episode highlighted the new level of scrutiny that he and the team would find themselves under as the first top-tier Australian cycling team to join the UCI WorldTour.

The team soon corrected any misconceptions about their commitment by setting up Gerrans for overall victory at the Tour Down Under. The finish of the penultimate stage on Old Willunga Hill – the first hill-top finish in the Australian stage race's history – was as spectacular as anyone could have hoped, with Gerrans being pipped for the stage win by Spaniard Alejandro Valvderde.

The Spaniard was taking part in his first race

since returning from a doping suspension, but it was Gerrans who claimed the ochre leader's jersey.

Gerrans's eventual overall win carried extra weight after his national title in Ballarat the week before, and set him up as one of the key riders to watch once the WorldTour peloton returned to Europe for the build-up to the first major Classic, Milan-San Remo.

It also helped boost the value of GreenEdge to potential sponsors. As the first WorldTour event of the season, every team wanted to leave Australia with something to show for their efforts. For GreenEdge, the best way to justify their presence in the peloton and earn the respect of their rivals was with a winning ride. Doing so in front of a home crowd and a worldwide television audience also repaid the faith of existing sponsors, and would help convince other sponsors to come on board.

Not that the second Tour Down Under win of Gerrans's career was all laced with smiles and bonhomie. A rival sports director, Sean Yates of Team Sky, questioned the condition of most of the GreenEdge riders, bar Gerrans and Cameron Meyer, on the final day of the race, raising the ire of the Australian team.

Yates was quoted as saying GreenEdge had 'not attacked the season in great shape' adding 'in general they are not in good enough condition. Obviously, to get in good condition you've got to train and be serious. Their state would suggest that's not been the case.' It was a bit like the coach of a beaten rugby team criticising the opposition's fitness only to be told to take a look at the scoreboard, mate.

Asked for his view on the critique after the race finish in Adelaide, GreenEdge sports director Matt White said: 'He's entitled to his opinion, but at the end of the day he has the team with the biggest budget in world cycling, and we won the bike race... I don't know why they are barking up that tree.'

The return to Europe was followed by a lull in the Belgian semi-Classics, including the one-day Kuurne-Brussels-Kuurne and Het Nieuwsblad, and the Strade Bianche in Italy, where the sceptics again emerged.

But good fortune soon returned, even though it came not from those who were expected to shine – like Goss, who deliberately started the season below the 2010 form that saw him win in the Bay Classic series and Tour Down Under and later at the Tour of Oman in February – but from other quarters.

Goss may still have enjoyed a three-day spell in the blue leader's jersey at Tirreno-Adriatico, but that came thanks to victory in the team time trial stage.

At Milan-San Remo, where Goss had taken victory in 2011, it was instead that man Gerrans again, winning *La Primavera* ahead of Switzerland's Fabian Cancellara. Gerrans's victory was initially attributed to opportunism, sitting on Cancellara's wheel as the pair led the race down the Poggio and into the final two kilometres. But as physiological data of Gerrans released by the team later showed, his power output as he raced to victory indicated that he'd used every ounce of strength to win the day. Fifteen times in the final seven kilometres, the Australian recorded power outputs that exceeded 1,000 watts.

Gerrans's victory was a huge statement of intent to those who doubted the WorldTour newbies. It meant GreenEdge had two Milan-San Remo champions on the books, the other being Goss, who won for HTC-Columbia in 2010.

The image of Gerrans crossing the finish line with arms aloft in the Australian champion's jersey symbolised exactly the lofty ambitions of the new team. Gerrans was not just the second Australian to win *La Primavera*, but the third Australian to win one of cycling's five 'monuments'. Milan-San Remo joins the Tour of Flanders, Paris-Roubaix, Liège-Bastogne-Liège and the Tour of Lombardy as the one-day Classics everyone wanted to win.

Gerrans – whose career includes stage wins in the Tour de France (2008), Giro d'Italia (2009) and Vuelta a España (2009) and overall victories in the Tour Down Under (2006, 2012), Tour of Denmark (2011) and the Herald Sun Tour in Australia (2005, 2006) – could not hide his joy if he'd wanted to.

As he drove home to Monte Carlo from San Remo following the podium ceremony and media interviews, Gerrans returned my call after I'd watched the race live in Australia, where it was 3.45am.

'This is definitely the biggest win of my career,' he told me. 'But to win it racing for an Australian team, and in the Australian champion's jersey, is perfect. There's nothing better you can do... It doesn't matter what happens to us now in the [European] spring because after winning one of the monuments, anything else will be a bonus. We have won one of the biggest races you can win, but we'll still be doing our best.'

But 'our best' clearly wasn't good enough to calm the doubters when a lull in success followed. GreenEdge repeatedly said during their formative months that the spring Classics in April would be a major focus. However, they all came and went with GreenEdge missing from the results, with the situation made all the worse when their in-form rider, Dutchman Sebastian Langeveld, broke his collar bone in a crash at the Tour of Flanders – a race in which he'd finished fifth the year before.

Arguably the most poignant result in 2012 for a GreenEdge team with one eye on the future was in the Circuit de la Sarthe stage race in France, where rookie Australian pro Luke Durbridge won the time trial and the overall classification.

In his first road race in Europe for GreenEdge since withdrawing from the Australian track endurance squad preparing for the London Olympics, Durbridge's victory in a race previously won by

Bernard Hinault and Greg LeMond, with only two team-mates in Weening and Eritrean rookie Daniel Teklehaimanot after Matt Wilson and Baden Cooke had dropped out, was a true measure of his potential and an example of the team's ability to win against the odds.

Their victory showed that Orica-GreenEdge had plenty to offer for the long term with its younger and developing riders.

And then there was the team's showing in the Vuelta a España, the final grand tour of the season. Not only did they get to cheer Simon Clarke's memorable stage win at Valdezcaray, where he outfoxed Tony Martin after a long break, but Clarke added the king of the mountains competition, which required him to be aggressive and opportunist enough to score points when the big-hitting climbers were not trading blows in the overall battle.

There was a moment of levity too. They reminded the peloton, and all who follow a sport so often bogged down in politics and controversy, that you can have a laugh now and again. The Orica-GreenEdge Vuelta squad's lip-sync video of the *Call Me Maybe* song became one of the most celebrated feats of the year and a YouTube hit – and justifiably so.

Coming at the tail end of a year that also saw Gerrans win the Grand Prix of Quebec in Canada before the WorldTour finished with the Tour of Beijing, their YouTube video brought some long-

overdue relief and joy at a time when cycling was
dealing with the ongoing controversies concerning
Lance Armstrong and the UCI.

In that, Orica-GreenEdge had done cycling a
much needed service – not that they would want that
to be their legacy. Winning still helps.

ADDENDUM

With the season almost over, the long-awaited report
into doping by Lance Armstrong and the US Postal
Service team was released by the United States Anti-
Doping Agency.

The consequences were far-reaching and Orica-
GreenEdge was not untouched.

Matt White, the team's head sports directors,
issued a personal statement in which he confessed
to having doped while a rider at US Postal Service
between 2001 and 2003.

His confession came after he was named in the
testimony made to USADA by Floyd Landis, one of
his former US Postal Service team-mates.

As we all now know, Armstrong did not defend
himself against the charges and so was found guilty
by USADA of the charges against him.

Armstrong was banned for life and stripped of
his seven Tour de France titles and all other race
results since August 1998.

USADA's findings were also ratified by the UCI.

White stood himself down from his positions as head sports director of the Orica-GreenEdge team and as Cycling Australia's professional co-ordinator as well as resigning his role as men's road coach as soon as he confessed to doping.

Cycling Australia then announced his contract was terminated, while his future at Orica-GreenEdge hinged on talks between team owner Gerry Ryan and general manager Shayne Bannan that were scheduled to take place in late October.

Rupert Guinness is the cycling writer for the *Sydney Morning Herald* (Fairfax). He has been covering the sport since 1986. Guinness, who now lives in Sydney, has covered every major cycling race – including 24 Tours de France – and still returns to Europe to cover races regularly. He has also authored 12 books, his most recent being *The Tour – Behind the Scenes of Cadel Evans' Tour de France* (Hardie Grant, 2012).

4

As his friends retire one by one, **David Millar** knows it will inevitably be his turn one day.

But the end of Michael Barry's career felt more poignant than most for David.

Like many of their generation, the two friends had shared experiences darker than they had bargained for – David very publicly, Michael in secret.

And so, as the embers of 2012 and Barry's career flickered, their training rides took on an even more reflective feel...

GONE BIKING

BY DAVID MILLAR

Most mornings start the same way these days: Archibald wakes up at 7am, my wife and I feed and change him, then we go down to breakfast where I have a coffee before messaging Michael Barry (unless he's beaten me to it). 'Biking?'

About an hour-and-a-half later, I'm setting off from the house to the road where his route from Girona meets mine from Cornella. It's a nice start for both of us, and although we live almost 20 kilometres apart, we both live at the top of hills, so those first few minutes are fast and invigorating and, somehow, almost without fail, we seem to always meet around the same point. This is remarkable, as I've become rather *laissez-faire* regards my departure times in my more mature age; we must both be living the exact same amount of *laissez* to our *faire* for it to work out every time.

It is a one kilometre dead-straight stretch of road where we tend to meet. I can see his catlike physique with its professional, piston-like pedal stroke approaching. It's a sight I've grown used to and one that always puts a smile on my face. More often than not, it is me who does the U-turn and we head off inland, deciding where we'll go as we pedal.

Yesterday was the first time Michael wasn't in his trade team kit. Retirement from racing has arrived, and with it the need to be sponsor-correct at all times on the bike. It was strange for both of us. We stopped at our regular café and, as we sat down, Michael said, 'It's odd to think this is all cycling will ever be for me from now on. I like it.'

'I suppose on the bright side there aren't many people in Toronto who'll be able to drop you. Well, at first anyway,' I replied.

It's less than two months until Michael and his family leave Girona, the home they've made over the past ten years, and return to Toronto. It's his childhood home, but it will be the first time he's lived there in almost 20 years.

This is happening to more and more of my friends. I was one of the first to turn pro out of all of us, and so have seen more come and go than most, but it's only now that I am so near the end of my racing career that I feel every retirement more personally. I know I'm an old pro because every time I come through the following caravan in a race I seem to know each *directeur sportif* as somebody I raced with, an old *guerrier* of the peloton. In 1997, each *directeur* seemed so old and scary. I suppose I'm old and scary now.

Michael and I used to always talk about the long-ago past (Michael's a natural raconteur, and I'm sure I've heard many of his stories at least three times) or the immediate future. Our racing was never a subject we needed to talk about. Until now that is.

Now all we seem to talk about is what happened to us and the sport, what we lived through and the mistakes we made. I try to help him come to terms with it all. It's important for Michael that he can ride with me at the moment because I'm the only person that he can speak to who has been through what he is going through and come out the other side.

It's a lifetime ago that we were teenage boys racing around our favourite roads, dreaming of one day being in the Tour de France – me in Hong Kong while Michael was in Toronto. Now it breaks our hearts to imagine having to tell those boys what they would end up going through, and I suppose we wouldn't tell them even if we could. We may have been through the mill but, for better or worse, it's made us who we are.

That is probably what is hardest to explain to people; they only see us as old professionals, the guys who doped, who cheated. That's true – that is who we are and we did do that – but I know how innocent we once were, how the dream was all-encompassing, powerful enough to transport us to a foreign land and a very foreign world.

There's not much of that innocence left, but the

older we've got, and the further time distances us
from our doping, the more we're able to rediscover the dreams we once had. The difference is that
now, with age and experience, our dreams come with
memories.

Cycling has taken us all over the world. We've
lived in different cultures and somehow picked up
different languages, made a multitude of different
friends and seen some of the most beautiful land-
scapes in the world. We've pushed ourselves beyond
what we ever thought was possible, be it freezing
down mountain passes in snow and rain thinking
we're going to be shaken off the bike from shiver-
ing so much, with hands too numb to even find the
brake levers, let alone pull them, to racing through
desert plains in 50-plus degree heat, convinced passing out from the heat would be nicer than melting.
And that's just the weather.

We'll miss the racing. We're racing cyclists after
all. That feeling of being in a peloton of professionals where you know you'll all make it round that
corner at 80 kilometres per hour side by side. Or
the adrenaline buzz you get trying to position your
sprinter in the final few kilometres of a grand tour
stage, waiting for gaps to open, willing them to open,
then squeezing through shouting at each other, 'Go!
Go! GO!' Then there's the focus before a prologue,
knowing there is no margin for error, having the
ability to hide from the wind while balancing the

need for speed with the limitations of your body and reconciling the fact that a crash could happen so easily even though you've imprinted every corner into your mental map.

The crashes we won't miss. There are more now than there once was; every race will see somebody breaking bones. Michael has been operated on twice this year: the first in February when he broke his leg and his elbow, then in August when he broke his arm. I broke my collarbone in March. We're getting too old for that kind of shit.

Yet what I think we'll miss most is the camaraderie. Grand tours are the best for that, especially a good old-fashioned Giro d'Italia where we spend almost more time in the team bus than we do on the road. We get to know each other so well and share such extreme experiences, from unbridled euphoria to the dark depths of fatigue-induced depression, that there's an intimacy about it all which is hidden behind joking and piss-taking.

As cyclists, we're inherently loners. I wasn't a team-sports player growing up; it simply never appealed to me. I much preferred going out alone on my bike for a few hours and imagining I was Miguel Indurain at the Tour de France or Maurizio Fondriest attacking on the Poggio. So to find myself years later on the brink of retirement, realising I'll miss the team spirit most, is a surprise.

Then there's the doping. Most of my peers did it

at one time or another. It was part of the sport back then, and contrary to the generations before who had also done it, we are the ones that live with the public knowledge that we did it.

The cleaning up of the sport has meant that we have found ourselves being confronted with our pasts and having to accept and admit what we did. This wasn't easy. It took a police arrest to get me to do it, and it took a federal investigation in the United States for Michael to do it.

It was, and I hope it will remain, the hardest experience of my life admitting to having cheated through doping. It was also the making of me. It has given me a purpose to everything I do, and the responsibility I feel towards cleaning up cycling has made me a better person. I regret massively that I ever crossed the line, and I feel anger towards the state of cycling back then that it could have happened to me, and so many others to whom doping had been such a disgusting thing.

Too many of us doped. Some were bad guys, but most were good guys who made the wrong choices. Then there were the special few who never crossed the line. Unfortunately there are not many of them left in the sport to tell us about their experiences.

These are the things Michael and I talk about now on our rides. The joviality is gone for the time being as we try to reconcile our pasts with the sport's future. I've been through this for years now, and so has Michael, although his has been locked behind closed doors; the exorcism has just properly begun for him.

The sport has changed through our hard work these past few years. It has been the regret of our experiences that has fuelled it, and our knowledge of how it happened and how to prevent it that has made it possible. If Michael and I arrived from Toronto and Hong Kong now, we would have a career that would have matched our youthful idealism. Others will get that chance now, and I'm very proud to have contributed to making that a reality.

I enjoy riding my bike now more than ever, and that is mainly due to Michael Barry showing me that a bicycle is more than just a racing machine. I'm going to miss those morning 'Biking?' messages.

David Millar was born in Malta in 1977 to Scottish parents. He got into cycling while living in Hong Kong in the early 1990s and turned professional for a French team in 1997. He has won stages and worn the leader's jerseys in all three grand tours. Arrested for doping in 2004 and subsequently banned for two years, he became an anti-doping advocate on his return to the sport and has been a member of the WADA Athlete Committee since 2008. His bestseller *Racing Through the Dark* was published in 2011.

5

After winning the 1997 edition of Paris-Roubaix, the French rider Frédéric Guesdon faced a long career chasing his next big win.

Although it came, at Paris-Tours in 2006, it was the Hell of the North that remained number one in the Frenchman's heart right up until the end of his career.

James Startt charts Guesdon's final journey to the famous, old stone showers at the Roubaix velodrome.

THE COBBLER RETIRES

BY JAMES STARTT

Few cyclists bother to go to the stone shower block once they've finished Paris-Roubaix these days, and even fewer champions go, preferring to clean the grit and grime from their bodies in the relative warmth and comfort of the team bus. But a handful of journalists still wait patiently beside one shower stall in the Roubaix velodrome, knowing that at least one of the race's heroes will eventually arrive – Frenchman Frédéric Guesdon.

Year in and year out, Guesdon would seek out his shower stall – the one with the gold plaque, which reads, 'Frédéric Guesdon, 1997' – after finishing yet another gruelling edition of the Paris-Roubaix cobbled Classic. It is tradition that each winner of the race has his own stall with his own plaque. And Guesdon has his.

But, in 2012, the journalists understood that, even more certainly than any other year, Guesdon would show up sooner or later, with this year's Paris-Roubaix marking his last ride as a professional.

And, finally, he arrived.

Well after the last television interview in the velodrome that hosts the race finish every year, and well
after entertaining a visit from the fervent supporters
of his fan club, Guesdon entered the showers, eyed
up his plaque, and entered the stall. Then, he placed
his duffel bag on the edge and took a deep breath.
Most of the other cyclists had already showered and
rejoined their team buses. Guesdon was in no hurry.

Twenty years after riding his first Paris-Roubaix
as an amateur, Guesdon wanted to savour the final
moments of the race that made him. Like other Paris-
Roubaix winners before him – such as the Frenchman Gilbert Duclos-Lassalle, Italy's Franco Ballerini
and Belgian rider Johan Museeuw – he chose to pay
the race a final honour by closing his career there.

He spoke easily with those around him, the dust
still caked on his face after the 257.5-kilometre race.
Clearly, though, the emotions were stronger than
any words. Most asked how Guesdon lived his last
day as a bicycle racer. But Guesdon understood that
he would be remembered for a different edition of
Paris-Roubaix.

Known as 'The Hell of the North', Paris-Roubaix
gives few gifts. It is one of the most unforgiving races
in the world. But Guesdon is one of the lucky ones
– one of the few who have experienced a rare day of
grace on the cobbles and, through good fortune and
great racing, captured one of bicycle racing's most
coveted trophies.

Back in April 1997 few knew the third-year professional with only one victory to his name. And even fewer expected him to be a player, let alone the winner, when the riders burst onto the velodrome in Roubaix.

But Guesdon rode what can only be described as the perfect race, entering the velodrome with a lead group of eight riders. Then, jumping early, he launched his sprint on the back straight, and simply rode away from his competition.

Behind the finish line, photographers focused and shot off a round of images as the Française des Jeux rider screamed across the line with both arms in the air. Few knew who he was. 'Sciandri?' asked one photographer, confusing Guesdon with his British team-mate Max Sciandri, who had been the team's designated team leader that day.

Many were even more confused when the thunder of the loudspeakers announced Guesdon's name. Guesdon, after all, had pulled off one of the greatest upsets in modern bike-racing history.

The next morning, *L'Equipe*'s headline read 'Guesdon Forever'. The words proved provident. In the 15-year career that followed, Guesdon rarely raced with such genius again. Yet no one could take away this one day of greatness.

'I know that page well,' Guesdon says of the French sports paper's leader. 'A copy of it is framed in my office. And it's true: for the rest of my career I was always known as, always announced as, the winner of Paris-Roubaix.'

For decades, Brittany, in the north-west region of France, has been known as a hotbed for cycling, and Guesdon was just one of countless children from the area that gravitated towards sport. But as he moved up through the ranks of cycling, Guesdon was different to most of the other adolescent hopefuls. Not for him the dream of winning the Tour de France, or of wearing the iconic yellow jersey. Instead he was attracted to the tough northern Classics, like Paris-Roubaix, or the equally gruelling Tour of Flanders in Belgium.

Racing for the Vélo Club Louison Bobet – an elite amateur club honouring one of the region's greatest champions – Guesdon first tasted the cobbles of Paris-Roubaix at the amateur version in 1992.

'I just remember thinking, "Okay, that was crazy – but not too crazy!"' Guesdon would return the next year, and every year after that, save for 1999 when an operation to remove a saddle sore forced him out of the spring Classics entirely.

Youth was on his side when he lined up at the start in Compiègne for the professional edition in 1997, and it was that very youth, coupled with his experience on the cobbles, that he used to his advantage at key moments during the day.

It is said that while Paris-Roubaix is hard to win, it can be lost at any moment. The nearly two-dozen cobbled sectors that punctuate the forlorn farm roads of northern France provide countless trappings. For that reason, Paris-Roubaix is usually reserved for experienced riders.

Guesdon lined up for every race he entered thinking of victory. In fact he was so optimistic on this occasion that he convinced team director Marc Madiot to make him one of the protected riders on the squad.

Perhaps because Madiot was a two-time winner himself, and understood that to win Paris-Roubaix a rider needs something not defined by Vo2 max tests or training logs. What they needed was the right attitude, and clearly Guesdon was already showing an abundance.

'At the start that morning, Max was to be our team leader for the day,' Guesdon remembers. 'But after him, I was also protected. In a race like Roubaix, the main objective is to stay near the front as long as possible.'

Under sunny spring skies and into a gentle headwind, Guesdon set out to do just that, riding near the front of the bunch. He punctured for a first time near the end of the first cobblestone section in Troisvilles. It is here where the race kicks into high gear, and every move becomes crucial to survival. Yet, despite the mishap, he didn't panic. Instead he remembered that there had been a crash behind him when the peloton had entered that first sector of cobbles, and that it had included his team-mate Sciandri. He knew that it meant there would be numerous riders chasing to return.

'With every section that went by, I remained with the leaders, and I came out of the Arenberg Forest in a good position,' Guesdon says about the treacherous section of cobbles that crosses the dismal forest at the edge of the forgotten mining town of Wallers.

But then, with about 40 kilometres remaining, Guesdon flatted again. Fortunately for Guesdon, however, Belgian Johan Museeuw had also flatted moments earlier. Just one year before, Museeuw had led his powerful Mapei team to the first-ever one-two-three sweep, and was eager to defend his title. Guesdon jumped in behind the Museeuw group and was soon shuttled back to the front.

'I flatted on a main road just as a big group was gaining ground. I thought then that my race was over. But Museeuw flatted and helped bring me back. Later that day Johan attacked in the Carrefour de l'Arbre section with Frédéric Moncassin and Andre Tchmil. I was in a group just behind. But then he flatted again! When we caught him, he was pretty un-nerved. He was determined to catch back up to the front. It's funny, but I have often said that Museeuw's bad luck was my good luck that day. He helped us catch Tchmil and Moncassin, and before I knew it we were heading to the velodrome for the victory!'

Entering the velodrome, Museeuw, Moncassin

and Tchmil were the favourites. Moncassin was clearly the fastest sprinter of them all, and had been second at the Tour of Flanders the week before. But he had also just been caught with Tchmil, while Museeuw had spent much of the day chasing.

Few were paying attention to Guesdon when he surprised them all with an early sprint. 'I just launched a crazy attack,' he says. 'I was young, and figured I had nothing to lose. Coming into the velodrome I was happy just to be in the front group, but there were a lot of guys faster than me on paper. But I was so excited to enter the velodrome with the front group, so I attacked from far out. It's funny, but if I'd had more experience I probably wouldn't have done something so crazy. And I probably wouldn't have won...'

'He had the sprint of a lifetime on the day it mattered most,' recalls his sports director, Madiot. But Madiot didn't see the actual finish from the team car. 'I just remember the day like an old film. All day long he rode well,' Madiot says. 'It was beyond real. Fifteen kilometres from the finish, I said, "You know, we can still win this thing!" It was like a premonition. But there is a difference between a premonition and reality. Right before the finish, the team directors' cars were diverted off the course and there was no more race radio because there can be no cars in the velodrome. So I didn't know what had happened. Then, from the edge of the velodrome, a mechanic from another team waved to me with both arms. At first I didn't understand. Then it hit me. The kid had just won Paris-Roubaix!'

'Everything was blurry after that,' Guesdon says of his greatest moment as a bike racer. 'The photographers, the crowd, stepping up on the podium, raising the cobble [the famous winner's trophy] above my head... It was just a big blur.'

Winning, it is said in bicycle racing, is one thing. Confirming success is quite another. And after winning Paris-Roubaix in the dawn of his career, Guesdon was soon faced with an even greater challenge – living up to that victory.

'You know, in some ways Gilbert Duclos-Lassalle is fortunate,' American champion Greg LeMond said in 1993. 'His greatest success came at the end of his career. He could really appreciate it.' The three-time Tour de France champion was speaking of his Gan team-mate who won Paris-Roubaix back to back in 1992 and 1993. LeMond, in contrast, finished his own career in a confused quagmire of illness and injury.

By winning such a big race so early on, Guesdon then faced an entire career of expectations. 'I won Paris-Roubaix in my first years as a pro, and then I had 15 years still to go,' he says.

'In the years that followed, I felt the pressure to live up to that expectation, although there was never as much pressure as at each subsequent Paris-Roubaix. That was the day that everybody expected great things – although I've got to say, I did too.'

Guesdon's challenge was made even more complicated by the rise of the mighty Mapei team, arguably the greatest Classics team in the history of the sport.

Back then, like today, Most big-budget teams invested in the media bonanza that is the Tour de France – but not Mapei.

Led by Belgian manager Patrick Lefevere, Mapei were one of the few exceptions. Instead, they put their money into recruiting the best Classics riders, and more specifically the men best equipped for Paris-Roubaix. In fact, Guesdon was the only rider to upset their winning reign at the race between 1995 and 2002 (Mapei was replaced as the team's main sponsor by Domo in 2001), and after 1997 Mapei took the top three spots at the race on two more occasions.

It was perhaps Guesdon's own manager, Marc Madiot, who best understood the Frenchman's true potential. 'Guesdon is not a great rider, but he will have some great rides,' Madiot said while returning from the 1998 Cholet Grand Prix in his team car.

His words proved prophetic. While Guesdon occasionally scored victories in minor races, he would have to wait nearly a decade until his next great win.

That day would come at the 2006 Paris-Tours one-day Classic – the historic autumn race that follows a route through the French heartland of the

Beauce region, through the Loire River Valley and finally into Tours.

Historically the race was nicknamed 'The Sprinters' Classic', as its flat roads lend themselves to a bunch gallop. But, in recent years, the addition of a series of short climbs on narrow roads near the finish have rendered the race more unpredictable.

Just like at the 1997 Paris-Roubaix, Guesdon didn't go into the race as the team leader. This time that honour went to a certain Philippe Gilbert, then an up-and-coming team-mate on Guesdon's Française des Jeux squad. But as Guesdon had already demonstrated, he often performed best in the shadow of others.

Just like at that '97 Paris-Roubaix, the race started under sunny skies, but this time with a slight tailwind. As happens most years, a lead group of riders crept away in the opening kilometres, and Guesdon was one of them.

'There were 28 of us and, although we never had a big gap, we worked well together,' Guesdon recalls. 'About 50 kilometres from the finish we started attacking, and I got into a group of four or five. But in the last kilometres, the peloton was closing in fast. They were about ready to catch us, and I attacked again. This time only Kurt-Asle Arvesen followed. I think he thought he had the faster finishing sprint but I think he was a little over confident.

'In the last kilometre, I let him lead. And he did

until 300 metres to go when I attacked – *et voilà*!'

Launching the sprint, Guesdon weaved across the Avenue Grammont, the historic finish of Paris-Tours, so that Arvesen wasn't able to profit from his slipstream.

Aversen won the under-23 road race at the 1997 World Championships in a sprint, and was known for his turn of speed. But again Guesdon's sprint came as a surprise, as he demonstrated the knack for having an exceptional ride on the days it mattered most.

Back in the team car, Marc Madiot, still Guesdon's director on the FDJ team, had had a vision. 'I knew he would win. It seemed impossible, but once again there was a film spinning in my head, and so I wasn't surprised.'

'You know, when I'm there for the win, I'm just able to ride above myself,' Guesdon says. 'Maybe I was a bit lucky at Paris-Roubaix, but at Paris-Tours there was no way I was going to lose. Finishing second just didn't interest me; it was winning or nothing at all.'

Victory at Paris-Tours served as a sort of bookmark in Guesdon's career after his early success at Paris-Roubaix. The two great Classics also served to define his career.

'The nine years in between were hard sometimes,' Guesdon admits. 'I won some races, sure, but I also had years with nothing. I did occasionally have some smaller races that gave me hope, but before I knew it, nine years had passed. There were times when I started asking myself questions, wondering if it was all worth it. But I always loved the sport. I never trained any less. I never had trouble getting out the door. I always came to the races prepared. That's the secret of longevity. And when you win at least sometimes, even smaller victories, you say to yourself, "I can still win, so maybe I can still get a big win."'

In the years that followed, Guesdon focused largely on shepherding young riders during their first years in the professional ranks. Only in his favoured Classics – the Tour of Flanders, Paris-Roubaix and Paris-Tours – did he ask to ride for himself. He proved to be a tireless road captain. Even as he approached his 40th birthday, there were few signs of tiring. But eventually he knew the time had come.

'I felt like 40 was a good age to stop. Plus more and more young riders were coming up and needed their own space. It made sense. Marc proposed finishing my career with Paris-Roubaix. Straight away, it sounded right.'

And so Guesdon went into the 2012 season excited to finish his career in a memorable manner. But what sounded right in the off-season turned immediately wrong as soon as 2012 was under way. After flying to Australia in January, Guesdon was caught in a crash in the final kilometre of stage one of the Tour Down Under. It was a mass pile-up that often happens as riders jostle for position before the final sprint. Little matter that Guesdon was simply using the race for training, he fell hard and broke his hip. Suddenly the romantic swansong on the Roubaix velodrome seemed an impossible dream.

But Guesdon was determined, and he used the setback as new motivation. 'Frankly, I thought my career was over in Australia,' Guesdon says now. 'But the accident gave me another challenge because I had never been in a position of being injured and absolutely wanting to be prepared for a certain objective. It was hard, but I don't regret it. And that is why I did it – so that I wouldn't have any regrets.'

Guesdon was obliged to remain hospitalised in Australia with his hip injury for a week before he could return to his native Brittany. It was then another six weeks before he even attempted to pedal his bike on a stationary home trainer. Finally, with little more than a month remaining until the start of Paris-Roubaix, Guesdon started training again. Suddenly he was in quite another kind of pursuit – that of regaining adequate condition to start his beloved race.

Guesdon had of course hoped to be competitive for his final 'Sunday in Hell', but after such chaotic preparation, he understood that he would be no better than operational for the race.

Paris-Roubaix is the most unforgiving race in the world, and leaves no margin for error. On the morning of the start, the Française des Jeux team surprised Guesdon by specially decorating the team cars in his honour for a right royal send-off. But the 2012 Paris-Roubaix – Guesdon's 17th professional start there – would prove to be the toughest yet.

Guesdon first lost contact with the bunch when he was caught in a crash midway into the race. As his group was regaining contact with the peloton, he punctured, just before the pivotal Arenberg Forest section of cobblestones.

'I had to wait a long time for a spare wheel, and then I just spent the rest of the day chasing.' For Guesdon, a one-time winner and frequent top 10 finisher, it was an unlikely position to be in. 'You know, in any other year I would have abandoned. But I knew this was my last Roubaix. I had to finish.'

And so, well behind the lead pack, Guesdon forged on. 'You know when you are feeling good that you wait for the cobblestones because you know it is the place to attack. But when you're hurting, you feel every stone, and you can't wait to get back on to the paved road.'

The road to Roubaix was long and painful but it was not entirely lonely. He covered the final kilometres, as farmland gives way to the sprawling suburbs that spill out from Lille, with one other rider, the Belgian Kristof Goddaert.

To this day, Guesdon does not know what place he finished because the two riders finished outside of the cut-off time. Bernhard Eisel, the 86th man across the line, was the last to be officially classified. He was 17 minutes 17 seconds behind the winner, Tom Boonen.

Guesdon followed a minute and 35 seconds after Eisel. In the finishing straight, Goddaert slipped back a little to allow Guesdon to say his farewells, just a modest and grateful wave to the appreciative crowd.

'It was a disappointing way to go out,' Guesdon admits. 'But it didn't matter.' He just wanted to finish, he says. He just wanted to see the velodrome one more time. And he just wanted to make it back to the showers – 'just one more time'.

James Startt has covered the Tour de France and other international bicycle races for 23 years and is the author of the first English history of the Tour de France entitled, *Tour de France/Tour de Force* (Chronicle Books), as well as numerous other cycling-related books. His photographs are distributed by Agence Zoom and are exhibited by the Agathe Gaillard Gallery, the oldest photography gallery in France. He has worked as the European Associate for *Bicycling* Magazine since 1999. Living in Paris, he currently holds the title, Our Man In Europe, for *Bicycling*.

6

Daniel Friebe explores how careful consideration of a rider's potential – sabermetrics, as it's called in baseball – is beginning to change the face of cycling, thanks to one team in particular.

Is the *Moneyball* theory about to alter professional cycling's relationship with statistics and finance?

CYCLONOMICS

BY DANIEL FRIEBE

It was tempting at the time to think that cycling's old guard had been frogmarched out of the building the day, in autumn 2006, when Giancarlo Ferretti became entangled in the world wide web.

Nicknamed the *'Sergento di Ferro'* – or 'Iron Sergeant' – Ferretti was a living, breathing monument to the *savoir-faire* that made professional cycling an art form long before it was to become a science. This was surely evolution's way of telling Ferretti that times were a-changing, and that his had come to its end. An internet scammer persuaded Ferretti that the telecommunications giant Sony Ericsson was ready to bankroll a new team to the tune of 11 million euros a year and Ferretti didn't wait to meet his new sugar daddies or sign the contracts before assembling his galaxy of stars.

Alas, six weeks later, Sony Ericsson's Stockholm-based 'head of sponsorship', Ron Westland, turned out to be a con-artist operating out of his bedroom in Tuscany. Ferretti had been merced, or Punk'd, or whatever the kids call it these days.

'It was all done via email, on this address that I now know must have been made up: ronwestlandsonyericsson@hotmail.com,' Ferretti lamented later. If it hadn't been quite so tragic – and wounded Ferretti to the extent that he has never returned to management – it would have been hilarious.

One of Ferretti's most illustrious acolytes, Alessandro Petacchi, recently said that, despite the precedent, 'Ferron' would have no trouble adapting to professional cycling today. Petacchi is probably right – not that much has changed... Not yet, anyway. The team car's indigenous species is still the ex-pro, admired, like he was in his racing days, for attributes usually surmised with a wistful look and thumb rubbing on forefinger, signifying something that the uninitiated just can't grasp. A good 'eye'. His tactical 'brain'. His *métier*. All that. Stuff you can't touch but which you know when you see it. Things that can be learned only in the sport of cycling's single Ivy League university – the peloton.

Baseball was once like this, too. But that all changed, famously, with Billy Beane and *Moneyball*. For those who haven't seen the movie, read the book or bought the T-shirt, a quick summary: a lavishly talented batter in his youth, Billy Beane spent half a decade floundering in Major League Baseball before deciding to reinvent himself as a scout, partly inspired by his own failures.

Beane found his calling at the Oakland A's – an

overspending, underachieving franchise soon to be dragged into an age of austerity by penny-pinching new owners. The pressure was on Beane and his colleagues to maintain if not improve on-field performances while spending a fraction of their old budget.

The solution to their seemingly impossible puzzle was something called sabermetrics. In a nutshell, it was all about statistics. But not any statistics. Certainly not the ones conventionally used by managers, coaches and fans to validate what they had already seen from the dugout, the bleachers or their armchair.

No, these were mind-bending numbers which completely changed the way that people understood baseball – at least the people who paid attention to them. The others claimed they didn't need sabermetrics: they knew a nice swing when they saw one, or a 90mph-plus fastball, or a fielder with hands like buckets and an arm like a rocket-launcher.

And what they couldn't see they gathered by browsing the stats – the ones put out by the people who ran the league and which never lied.

Only that was the point the sabermetricians had been arguing for a decade or two, before anyone with any influence had paid them any heed: those stats really did lie, at least about which performance parameters really did win and lose baseball matches. They also skewed the market to the degree that the

richest teams in baseball were forking out indecent
sums of cash for the wrong players. The guys with
good figures in the wrong categories, or who matched
the scouts' identikit of what baseball players ought
to look like. The results were a paradox: some of the
worst teams in baseball were some of the richest.

At the end of the 1990s, Billy Beane became the
driver and poster-boy of the Oakland A's' opposite
approach: they started spending less and winning
more. The reason was that they were spending wisely.
Under Beane, the scouts gradually ceded power to
the analysts, intuition bowed to evidence and art to
science. To the untrained eye, the A's looked like a
bargain bin full of whatever old jumble the rest of
the league had rejected; in reality – and the end-of-
season victory counts would bear this out – they were
a precious mosaic of gems that other team managers
had mistaken for useless rubble.

The A's would make the play-offs four seasons
in a row from 2000 to 2003, and set a Major League
Baseball record of consecutive wins in 2000. In 2004,
journalist Michael Lewis told their story in the book
Moneyball: The Art of Winning an Unfair Game.

By this time, Beane had many admirers, one
being a 46-year-old American telecommunications
magnate named Bob Stapleton. California born and
bred, Stapleton says that, in baseball terms, his family was 'split right down the middle' between the A's
and their neighbours and enemies the San Francisco

Giants. Stapleton declines to specify on which side of the Northern California divide his allegiances lay – but admits that Billy Beane is a 'brilliant, innovative guy'. So brilliant and innovative, in fact, that, when Stapleton took control of his own sporting franchise in 2007, Beane became 'the clear inspiration for our programme'.

Beane had set out to exploit inefficiencies in the market for players and the sport as a whole's conception of tactics. For five years, Stapleton would do the same, perhaps a little less systematically, but with even more success.

In *Moneyball*, Lewis estimates that every victory cost the Oakland A's in the region of half a million dollars. Meanwhile some teams were paying six times that amount, around $3million in wages, for each of their wins.

In cycling, Stapleton was able to create an even bigger discrepancy: between 2008 and his team closing in 2011, they notched 282 victories at an approximate cost of just over €100,000 apiece.

Contrast this with Ag2r La Mondiale, who in the same four-year period were shelling out €750,000 for each of their 43 race wins (admittedly slightly hamstrung by high French taxes). Or with Rabobank, whose 89 victory bouquets each came at a price of over €500,000. Or, indeed, with T-Mobile in 2006, who could muster only 16 wins at a combined cost of €15 million.

Of course there are other ways to gauge value in cycling besides race victories. Different teams and their sponsors have different *raisons d'être*: for some it's specific goals in selected races, for instance the yellow jersey in the Tour de France; for others it's the UCI team rankings, while for a third group it could simply be earning exposure for the logo on their jersey. Also, a stage win in the Circuit de la Sarthe can hardly be compared to overall honours in a major tour, which Stapleton's team never achieved. Nonetheless, few would argue that if Beane had an equivalent in cycling, 'Blue Chip Bob' was that man between 2007 and 2011.

* * *

One immediate parallel, besides their ties to California, was that Beane and Stapleton's teams had previously epitomised those 'market inefficiencies' that they would eventually try to exploit. Stapleton's first and main brief when he took over at T-Mobile in 2006, though, was to do with credibility, not efficiency; it just so happened that in ridding the team of its dopers and facilitators, Stapleton couldn't help but come across other, glaring weaknesses in the way T-Mobile had been run.

'Major investment, minimal results,' is his concise description of what he inherited. Within a few weeks of his arrival, he was waving away the protests of his *directeurs sportifs* and declaring a purge on the team's highest-paid, marquee names. One of those directeurs sportifs, Brian Holm, recalled: 'Bob just said, "Right, him, him and him have to go." We tried telling him that, no, Wesemann, Kessler and Klöden were the big German stars, they were untouchable, but Bob said we were wrong.'

Over the next few months, Stapleton would replace the old and established with the young and unproven while imposing blanket pay-cuts across his staff. The weird thing was that results improved almost immediately. To the question of 'How?', Holm responds succinctly: 'He whipped our arses.'

Stapleton, as you'd expect, provides a more nuanced explanation. In it are some fragments of what he had picked up from Beane. Others, Beane might have picked up on if he'd worked in cycling...

THE WISDOM OF THE CROWDS

In other words, the combined brainpower of a group will usually make better decisions than any of the individual components – particularly when the group is diverse. A classic example: in a competition to guess the weight of an ox, the average of all of the guesses will typically be much closer to the right answer than most if not all of the individual estimates. Stapleton and his team appreciated this and applied it to their policy on transfers.

'It would generally be a conference call led by team manager Rolf Aldag, in which all of the *directeurs sportifs* and I participated. Rolf would have a list of up to one hundred names and we would go through, one-by-one, listening to what everyone had to say and looking at the available data about each individual guy. Finally, at the end, we'd have a list of guys to talk to.'

DIVERSITY IS KEY

'The wisdom of the crowds' worked for Stapleton, as it tends to do when the components of the crowd are diverse. In a world where *directeurs sportifs* double as scouts (Stapleton: 'They're the only guys who can see inside the race, beside the riders; our *directeurs* were at races to manage the team but also to look for new riders'), there are also other reasons to assemble a staff with a broad base of knowledge, geographically speaking. In the team's best season, 2009, the team's brain trust comprised two Germans (Aldag and Jan Schaffrath), an Italian residing in Belgium (Valerio Piva), a Dutchman (Tristan Hoffman), an Australian (Allan Peiper), a Dane (Brian Holm) and Stapleton himself.

'We had all the best talent pools covered,' Stapleton says. Compare this with Liquigas, whose technical staff in 2009 was made up of four *directeurs* from one region of northern Italy (the

Veneto) and two from another (Lombardy). Other teams, like Cofidis and Lampre, are similarly centralised (read parochial), and either recruit heavily from a single region in which their *directeurs* specialise (for Cofidis, north-east France, for Lampre north-west Italy) or rely on friends and acquaintances, often former team-mates from their own racing career, as further field for intelligence. Which is fine... except that it doesn't work nearly as well.

'If a guy is recommended by a third party, he ends up talking to me, who isn't from his country, who he doesn't know, and who has never seen him race. It goes without saying that, say, a young Australian deals with Allan Peiper, who everyone in Australian cycling knows,' says Stapleton's former team manager Rolf Aldag.

'The problem isn't identifying the talent. With a guy like Edvald Boasson Hagen, the ability's obvious, but that means it becomes a problem to get the guy, because there's competition. And that's where we were good, also because we had a history of turning young guys like Mark Cavendish into big successes.'

SHOP FOR GUYS WITH WARTS

Shop for guys with warts. Er, excuse me? Warts? Yes, warts, as in Billy Beane's shorthand for imperfections, which turn out to have little or no bearing on a rider's ability to perform. A 'wart' could be physical, like the significant difference in the length of former HTC-Highroad rider Patrick Gretsch's legs, or it could be technical like Peter Velits's aberration of a riding position. Either way, it's either superficial or fixable – only other teams haven't grasped that, and so the rider is underpriced and underrated.

'Gretsch is a guy who wouldn't have got through a lot of teams' screening process, because the discrepancy between his two legs is quite radical. For us he was an easy hire,' notes Stapleton. Hayden Roulston was another one: best-known to some for what was reported at the time as a bar-room brawl in October 2005, in addition, the Kiwi had nearly been forced out of the sport by a heart condition the following year. He overcame that, miraculously, with Reiki massage, returned to racing and performed creditably with Cervélo in 2009 and 2010, but was still underpriced for a guy who two years earlier had been an Olympic silver medallist in the individual pursuit.

If Roulston went on to do well for Stapleton, Matt Goss did brilliantly. Stapleton says that the Aussie also had 'warts'. He laughs heartily. 'I mean, he was hardly a lesson in *souplesse* on the bike.' More to the point, Goss had also been under-appreciated and underused as a team leader at Saxo Bank, despite glimmers of precocious brilliance in his three years at the Danish team.

'Goss is a guy who was clearly, clearly undervalued when we took him,' confirms Aldag. Just over a year after joining HTC, Goss had won Milan-San Remo. A few months later he had signed for GreenEdge for around five times what Stapleton had paid.

The notion of 'warts' wasn't unique to, or invented by, Billy Beane. As Simon Kuper and Stefan Syzmanski point out in *Soccernomics*, in the 1970s and 1980s the Nottingham Forest management duo of Brian Clough and Peter Taylor used to actively seek out footballers with personal problems, knowing that they would generally come cheap. They would then work with the player to resolve whatever his particular issue was – often drink, women or gambling. If the potential on the pitch was there, no foible was too daunting – on one proviso: they had to be open about it, then let Clough and Taylor enlist whatever external help was required to fix their vice.

Boozers and betting fiends are rare in professional cycling (we'll leave the women for now), but there were still echoes of the football managers' technique in Beane's and Stapleton's approach.

'Whatever their particular issue was, we let them know that we would work with them on it, and had concrete plans to do that,' Stapleton says.

In many cases, he adds, knowing this exerted a stronger pull on a rider's motivation than the bigger cheque being waved by another team. Thus, HTC's limited spending power also became an effective filter, allowing them to recruit people for the right reasons.

'The guys coming to us were motivated for the right reasons – success and improving, not money,' says Stapleton. Whether some of the most cash-happy teams in the peloton in 2012 – BMC and Katusha perhaps – can say the same may be a moot point.

RISKY WARTS

There was only one kind of 'wart' that would instantly turn Stapleton off: anything in a rider's history or biological passport that indicated foul play. The majority of UCI WorldTour teams now scrutinise medical files in the same way – Sky even request a rider's SRM data for a whole month before making a commitment – while lower-ranked teams pay relatively meagre sums for high-risk, high-flyers returning from doping bans.

'An obviously clean biological passport is worth much more than a more dubious one,' says Italian rider agent Alex Carera.

Indeed, it is widely known on the pro scene that one major team was very close to signing Alessandro Ballan in March 2009 – but called off the deal having examined his bio passport (coincidentally or not, an Italian magistrate in Mantova later hypothesised that Ballan had undergone a blood transfusion that very month).

BMC wound up getting Ballan for a relatively modest fee for a rider who, at the time of the negotiations, was the reigning world champion. They soon paid for the gamble, though, when the Mantova investigation came to light early in 2010, causing them to diplomatically suspend Ballan for the entire Classics season.

Stapleton's ace recruiters, of course, disbanded with HTC-Highroad at the end of 2011, but he can take heart from the knowledge that even the ones no longer managing teams retain fully functional wart detectors. Rolf Aldag attended the 2012 Tour of Switzerland in his role as Omega Pharma-Quick Step's technical consultant. One day early in the race, the German stood shooting the breeze with some friends.

'The first guy I'd sign is Fredrik Kessiakoff,' he told them. 'Really good mountain biker, got great results when he started on the road, had that Epstein-Barr virus for a year or so, and is starting to go well again, but will still be really cheap...'

The next day, Kessiakoff beat Fabian Cancellara to win the 34.3-kilometre time trial in Gossau. A few weeks later he'd be one of the unsung stars of the Tour de France, attacking incessantly in the mountains, and a few weeks after that he'd win another time trial at the Vuelta a España. Aldag claims that he would have snapped up the Swede, warts and all, way back in June.

'If a guy's shown something once, and there's a good and temporary reason why he's no longer performing at that level, that's a guy worth gambling on, because the financial risk is very small.'

EXPLOIT MARKET FORCES

Sometimes a team manager doesn't need to look for 'warts' to get bang for his buck. Sometimes quite fickle market forces create opportunities – and it's up to savvy team managers to exploit them. For example: at around the time when Stapleton arrived on the men's pro scene – and for several years before that – sprinters were bafflingly underpriced. So, at least, says Alex Carera.

'They were regarded in the same way as goalkeepers in football: you had to have two in a squad, but signing them was really a box-ticking exercise for most teams; consequently they were pretty cheap.'

It could have been something to do with Lance Armstrong hoovering attention and therefore resources towards major tours; it could have been the erstwhile UCI ranking system's limited rewards for stage wins in smaller races; whatever it was, when Stapleton and his *directeurs* decided that aiming for overall honours in major tours was risky, expensive and maybe impossible without doping, they discovered that the alternative of a sprint- and time-trial-focused team was, by comparison, both cheap and dependable. Between them, in 2008, sprinters Mark Cavendish, Gerald Ciolek, André Greipel, Edvald

Boasson Hagen and Greg Henderson cost Stapleton less than €1,000,000 – but won him 43 races. Sixteen wins that year also came in time trials. Good luck, though, to any manager attempting to load his team with speed in the same way today.

'The new rankings system has changed everything. Sprinters bring in a lot of points, and consequently have become a lot more expensive,' says Carera.

THE UNITED NATIONS OF SUCCESS

A year after bowing out of professional cycling, Bob Stapleton is making his money in much the same way that he made winners at HTC-Highroad: with shrewd investments.

'I'm doing some private equity stuff. I think I'm better at that than managing a sports team...' he says. Stapleton is being falsely modest. He knows that the team he created may have been the most cost-effective in cycling history, and he also has clear ideas about how they mastered the market. But if he had only one piece of advice for another team hoping to emulate HTC-Highroad's success, he says, it would be to strive for a cosmopolitan mix, not just because several 'talent pools' will harbour more treasures than one, but 'because this overrides any dominant subcultures within the team'.

He explains: 'Sometimes we were going to races with something like 16 nationalities represented between riders and staff, and people left their national biases at home. They were in a new environment, decisions were being made based on merit, and for whatever reason the international element added to the chemistry. People felt it was more special, they felt they were really surrounded by the best, plucked from all over the world. Once you had no more than five or six guys from any nationality in the team, you didn't have any dominant subculture, so then the culture of the team became the strongest thing.'

All of which could easily have been plundered straight from a management textbook – except the results plead in Stapleton's favour. It's also notable that some of the consistently worst-performing teams in professional cycling are among the most homogeneous, with four of the bottom six-ranked teams in the 2012 UCI team rankings drawing two thirds or more of their roster from a single country (Euskaltel, FDJ, Lampre and Ag2r).

Of course lack of money more than lack of diversity may be these teams' main handicap, and there may also be pressure from sponsors to favour 'home riders', but they could, equally, be helping themselves by casting their net wider.

Stapleton recognised early that the existence of several teams or one very rich one in certain countries could inflate the demand for, and hence the price of, riders there. His team never signed a single French rider – not, he says, 'because of any bias against them, but because they were very in demand from French teams, and so became very expensive for what you were getting'.

The same phenomenon can also have a negative impact on riders' motivation in certain environments. Raimondo Scimone, an Italian agent who represents the interests of a number of Russian riders, suggests that the Katusha team and its massive investment may have stunted the growth of some athletes from that country.

'I've seen it with a few guys,' he says. 'They seem to take it for granted that there'll be a place for them at Katusha, and it becomes a comfort zone for them. Conversely, foreign teams don't even bother going after the young Russian guys, because they just assume that they'll end up at Katusha. But it could be that a Russian would actually be much better in one of those teams.'

It's perhaps no coincidence, then, that Russians accounted for just under half of Katusha's roster in 2012 but fewer than a quarter of their wins. Or, indeed, that Yuri Trofimov, Denis Menchov,

Footnote At the time of writing, Scimone had more on his mind than his underperforming Russians: according to *La Gazzetta dello Sport*, a Padua magistrate suspected the agent and sports doctor Michele Ferrari of conspiracy to launder money, tax evasion and facilitating doping. Scimone admitted that he was under investigation but strongly denied the allegations.

Alexandre Kolobnev – in fact, pretty much every
Russian with any pedigree prior to joining the team –
has scored fewer victories and fewer ranking points
since signing with Katusha.

PAOLO TIRALONGO: SELF-PUBLICIST EXTRAORDINAIRE

Other pitfalls to avoid are more subtle, but equally
intriguing. In both *Soccernomics* and *Moneyball*, the
authors argue that sports clubs are beholden to often
unconscious 'sight-based prejudices' – for example,
an irrational and unsubstantiated preference for players who are particularly stylish or athletic or just 'look
the part'.

Sometimes it's simpler even than that: one top
English football club started to notice that scout-
ing reports were irrationally, disproportionately
biased towards blond-haired players, presumably
because they were more conspicuous and memorable. Psychologists call this the 'availability heuristic'
– a mental short-cut based on the premise that the
easier something comes to mind, the more important it must be.

This applies in cycling, too. For example, says
Scimone, Denis Menchov was always a relatively
hard and modestly-valued sell for a multiple grand
tour winner, even before his name was mentioned in
connection with various doping scandals.

Scimone suspects that this has as much to do

with Menchov's non-existent media profile as with
something else: 'You never see him in the race. I'm
his agent, I sit there watching races on TV, looking
for him all the time, but I never see him.

'Whereas someone like Paolo Tiralongo
is never off your screen because he's invariably riding next to and chatting with his mate
Alberto Contador. I'm sure that also has an
impact on Tiralongo's value.

'Similar with Pippo Pozzato: okay, he's got the
media profile, but he's also very stylish on the bike.
He stands out... even though he can't win a race even
if someone's pushing him.'

CHANGING THE GAME

So far, using Bob Stapleton and HTC-Highroad as
our case study, we've looked at several ways in which
a cycling team turned the ignorance or inefficiencies
of competitors to their distinct advantage.

Billy Beane had gone a step further, leaning
heavily on analytical data to not only guide
recruitment but, before that, to shift a paradigm, to
change the way a game of baseball was played and
understood.

In cycling, for now, this appears to be uncharted territory, for all that Team Sky and their performance analyst, Tim Kerrison, have to some extent
debunked conventional wisdom about how to win

the Tour de France, at least with a certain type of rider, with a tactic clearly grounded in empirical analysis. Its most obvious, defining characteristic: attacking and responding to attacks was a waste of energy.

'If we're going at 450 watts up a climb, it takes 500 watts to go away, and we know that no one can sustain that on a 20-minute climb,' Bradley Wiggins explained during the Tour. In Beane's mind, batters and pitchers were reduced to numbers, their vital stats, and it's not too much of a stretch to imagine that, for Team Sky principal Dave Brailsford now, they become wattages.

The challenge in both cases is keeping emotion out of it. For coaches like Beane, to quote *Moneyball* author Michael Lewis, 'winning is simply a matter of figuring out the odds and exploiting the laws of probability... To get worked up over plays, or even games, is as unproductive as a casino manager worrying over the outcomes of individual pulls of the slot machines'.

Brailsford obsessively pores over the best publicly-available resource for cycling results and statistics, the Dutch-run website cqranking.com. Using numbers from the site, he also draws up his own 'expected value' graphs plotting rider ages against their rankings; young riders who fall below the required standard (like Chris Froome at the end of his first year with Team Sky, as noted by *Cycle Sport* magazine at the time) may be granted a stay of execution, but anyone still underperforming as they near and enter their thirties is quickly culled.

'Those guys, you get rid of them straight away,' Brailsford has said in the past. It's tempting to assume that the 35-year-old Spaniard Juan Antonio Flecha fell foul of this rule of thumb at the end of the 2012 campaign, given that, as Billy Beane told Simon Kuper, the author of *Soccernomics*, 'Nothing strangulates a sports club more than having older players on long contracts, because once they stop performing, they become immovable.

'And as they become older, the risk of injury becomes exponential. It's less costly to bring a young player in. If it doesn't work, you can go and find the next guy, and the next guy. The downside risk is lower, and the upside much higher.'

Measuring an athlete's rate improvement or decline over time is easy in cycling, of course. All you need to do is monitor his power outputs with an SRM meter and possibly their other physiological data, in races, training or lab tests. Easy... or it is if he's already one of your riders. Screening for prospective new signings on the basis of more than just their results and subjective judgement is more tricky, but some are trying.

Garmin chief Jonathan Vaughters claims to trawl the internet for live streams of races from all over the world, around the clock, for the purposes of identifying new targets. Vaughters also says that it pays to be discerning.

'For example, the Ronde de l'Isard stage race in France is seen as one of the showcases for under-23 riders, and a lot of teams recruit on the basis of who does well there, but there can be big variations between two editions of the race. They tend to do a lot of the same climbs year after year, so you can time them, work out their climbing speed or VAM [vertical metres gained per hour] and compare year on year,' Vaughters says. He also uses other gauges, he says, that he is not at liberty or willing to disclose.

Our sense, though, is that even teams in the vanguard like Team Sky and Garmin may only be scratching the surface. Not that it's surprising or their fault, especially not when a much richer sport like professional soccer has only recently begun substituting grizzled old scouts in flat caps with computer nerds who have never kicked a ball.

In the mid-1990s, a handful of visionary managers across Europe, including the Frenchman Arsène Wenger and the Norwegian Egil Olsen, were already using primitive match analysis software, but it was only when management consultancy Opta began logging and publishing data for Premier League matches in 1996 that the geeks started to reach a wider audience.

Today Opta employs well over 100 people, has offices in London, Munich, Milan, Madrid, Montevideo and New York, and logs data for thousands of matches every weekend. As of two years ago, they are also involved in cycling, computing the IG Pro Cycling Index on behalf of spread-betting company IG Markets.

The aim of that is to offer a better answer to the question of who is the world's greatest cyclist than the official, UCI equivalent – but Opta could one day provide a much more extensive and more useful range of statistics on bike racing.

In football, Premier League clubs driving the statistical revolution like Manchester City, Arsenal, Chelsea, Fulham and Liverpool employ up to eight analysts each, while still also relying heavily on customised data produced for them, at a price, by Opta. The search, though, for the holy grail – a statistic which would provide the ultimate gauge of an individual player's influence on a game – goes on. One day, assembling the best football team in the world could be as easy as looking down the first eleven names in a spreadsheet and finding the nearest available Emirates sheikh to finance their purchase.

In cycling, who knows what a company like Opta – or indeed an anorak in their bedroom – could one day come up with?

'I'd love a ranking of the kilometres every rider spends in breakaways throughout the course of a season. That would really help us,' says Gianni Savio, the manager of the Androni Giocattoli team. And what if such a league table proved irrefutably that breakaways were, on balance, a complete waste of a team's resources? Evidence like that could change bike races beyond recognition, just as some of Beane's discoveries have changed baseball. More likely, more mundanely, the stats would be misleading or inconclusive.

'Okay, it might be interesting to know that a guy gets in a lot of breaks, but just because he gets in breaks for one team, it doesn't mean that he'll be able to do it with another team. At HTC our guys were never allowed to go away,' says Rolf Aldag.

Nonetheless, there could surely be endless information that might give teams that knew how to use it an edge. For example, under which weather conditions is an attack on the Poggio most likely to succeed in Milan-San Remo? What percentage of sprints does Mark Cavendish win when he begins his acceleration 200 metres from the line, and what percentage when he lets rip from 250 metres? Sky and one or two other teams are already examining contingencies like this – albeit on a relatively small scale. But Duncan Alexander, the head of content at Opta in the UK and a long-time lover of professional cycling, can foresee a day when number-crunching plays a much bigger role in their decision-making.

'Cycling is interesting in that it's the ultimate sport, but it's only really the leaders who get to express their value in terms of results,' Alexander tells me.

'I think, consequently, most people know what the big stars can do. Where it could be much more interesting is with domestiques.

'It's very difficult to rate them with objective data at the moment. Sometimes, it seems to me, it's more a case of their perceived value being affected by who they know.

'We could do a lot more with cycling, but it relies on manpower and actually watching the races,' he continues. 'For example, for any good assessment of breakaways, you'd need to see whole stages, and they're not always broadcast.

'A lot of the action often happens in the first hour, which is only televised at major tours. But, yes, even if I'm biased, I do believe there would be value in it if a team decided to invest in analysis like the football clubs are now.

'For instance, if you know that if you cover an attack on the Poggio eight times of 10 that the race will finish in a sprint nine times out of 10, and you've got the best sprinter, it becomes very interesting.'

THE DEVIL'S IN THE DATA

So how far will the trend develop, and how quickly? Well, the Sky approach has already turned even some conservative heads, although not every other team has the means or intelligence to mimic Dave Brailsford. It seems likely that Brailsford, Kerrison and Sky's other coaches will continue to lead the way in terms of data-guided race strategy – not that they will always tell us what they're up to.

'The problem with all of this is that, if someone does latch on to something, everyone follows and the advantage is lost,' notes Alexander. What we do know is that, if Stapleton was inspired by Billy Beane and the Oakland A's, for what it's worth, so is Brailsford.

'What he did was take a really refreshing, clean review of the standard thought processes that had developed over a period of God knows how long,' Brailsford said of Beane in *Cycle Sport*. 'In baseball, they talk about a player having "the full set" if they are good at certain things, but to have someone come in and say, "Are we measuring the right things?" was refreshing... Beane stood back and said he wasn't going to go with conventional wisdom. Baseball does lend itself fantastically to stats, much more so than road racing, but I do think it's refreshing that there was an industry where everyone thought in one way until a guy came along and said, "Hang on a minute."'

The bad news is this: the incentive to employ any such lateral thinking was largely undermined when the UCI introduced the WorldTour in 2011. Under the system, rankings points scored by a team's riders the previous season become the *sine qua non* for entry into the most prestigious races, even if those points were amassed in a different jersey. This throws up the potential for farcical scenarios like Euskaltel's rumoured move for the newly-retired Oscar Freire and his stockpile of points at the end of 2012 – even if Freire had no intention of racing in 2013. Perhaps more to the point, according to Bob Stapleton it has created an 'inefficient market' – a false meritocracy that flatters the rich and penalises the poor. Star academies like HTC-Highroad, says Stapleton, are being hustled out of the sport because the WorldTour system takes all emphasis away from rider development and also teamwork.

'You can't afford to take a bunch of young guys and build them up like we did, because that's a whole load of riders in your team with no points,' Stapleton argues.

'The system plays right into the hands of the super-rich: the Katushas, the BMCs, the Skys. It also defeats the principal of teamwork; an individual rider can't focus on working for the team, because he knows he might finish the season with no points and no value. It's the death of the team-mate. I had a ton of arguments with Pat McQuaid about this, because it totally undermined the stability of our team. If you ask me, if you want people to cheat, this is also the best advert for it. It totally gutted the fundamental goals of our team.'

And, to an extent, gutted the application of any *Moneyball*-inspired method of recruitment in cycling. Suddenly, in the scrap for starting berths in the major tours and the Classics, only one number matters: a rider's ranking points.

A decade ago, Cofidis owner François Migraine was widely mocked for his obsession with a previous incarnation of the UCI rankings. Some riders – the Spaniard Bingen Fernandez was one that Migraine often name-checked – earned a contract and made a career out of sprinting for top 20 or top 30 finishes and the accompanying ranking points. Like we said, other team owners and managers laughed. Now they are reduced to doing the same.

'The contracts being signed by riders these days are heavily, heavily linked to how many points they've got. You can almost put a dollar number on every point,' says Stapleton.

To some fans, of course, this will make no odds. Billy Beane's rationalisation of what was a highly emotive, often illogical melting pot of variables, like all sports, was in itself deeply unromantic; what's the difference, they'll say, if suddenly players or riders or whatever are being selected on the basis of one numerical criterion, like, say, ranking points, rather than some whizz-bang formula concocted by a geek behind his computer?

And they'll be wrong, because the reason that *Moneyball* became such a hit, as a book and a film, and the reason that Michael Lewis wrote it, was that it contained a parable of enduring, universal and irresistible allure, regardless of the metaphor in which it is packaged: *Moneyball* was, you see, essentially the story of David outsmarting Goliath.

But partly thanks to the UCI, in cycling the nerds have largely been kept at bay. For a while yet, it looks safe for the old guard to re-enter the building.

A freelance journalist specialising in cycling, **Daniel Friebe** has covered 12 Tours de France and all the major races on the international calendar. He is the roving European Editor of *procycling* magazine. In 2008, Daniel collaborated with Mark Cavendish on the best-selling *Boy Racer* (Ebury Press). He is also the author of *Mountain High* (Quercus) and *Eddy Merckx: The Cannibal* (Ebury). Daniel has written on cycling, football, golf, cricket and tennis for publications including *The Daily Telegraph*, *The Sunday Telegraph*, *FourFourTwo*, *Spin Cricket Monthly* and *Outdoor Fitness* magazine.

7

Owen Slot charts the parallel rise of Australia's Anna Meares and Great Britain's Victoria Pendleton – an at-first friendly rivalry that threatened to turn ugly as the two stars rose, culminating in the ultimate showdown in the final of the track sprint at the 2012 Olympic Games in London.

PENDLETON VERSUS MEARES

BY OWEN SLOT

This story does not really start in Stuttgart in 2003, but, if you rewind that far, you find a place of pleasing innocence, the calm before the storm, two girls having a drink at the bar together. And no, of course, back then neither would have dreamed of how their lives would come to revolve around each other, how a nascent friendship could develop such a bitter taste, how together they would create a rivalry so epic it would raise their sport to unimagined heights.

At its most dramatic, in the cauldron of the 2012 Olympic year, their sparring on the pine tracks of the world's velodromes would become box office gold. But in 2003, at the World Championships in Stuttgart, Victoria Pendleton was 22 and Anna Meares was 19 – a Brit and an Aussie, two riders from opposite sides of the world, their competitive lives in front of them.

And at the end of those championships, when they had both finished competing, they had a beer together. Just a drink, nothing more. But in years to come, people – generally people in the media – would wonder how they could ever have shared even a moment's closeness, and whether they could ever be close again. The psychology of their rivalry was destined to be fascinating.

Something small and decent happened at the Stuttgart bar that night. One of the boys spilled his beer over the jacket that Meares was wearing and, in a nice moment of girly unity, Pendleton rescued her.

'No problem, don't worry,' Pendleton said, and took Meares down to the toilets to help her clean herself up. And that was all; then they were back out at the bar together. Two very decent people, neither yet with a world title to their name, twinned by a drink and a kind of a friendship and also vast, yet very differing, simmering competitive spirits.

In fact, their story really started a year earlier, at the Commonwealth Games in Manchester. That was when Pendleton first encountered Meares, though on that occasion there was not one Meares but two of them – Anna and her elder sister Kerrie.

It was Kerrie that Pendleton rode against there in Manchester, and not Anna. The young British rider nevertheless got an understanding of what the next 10 years would feel like.

Pendleton likes to think of herself as a clean rider, an athlete with an understanding and espousal of the concept of good sportsmanship. But she received a taste of what she would interpret as the other extreme when she rode against Kerrie in the individual sprint semi-final of those Commonwealths, when Kerrie, on her inside, rode her high up the steep banking of the Manchester velodrome track and used her bike to flick her against the boards.

That was just one race, just one tactic, yet the moment clearly made an enormous impression. A decade later, when Pendleton published her excellent autobiography, *Between the Lines*, she rewinds to those Commonwealth Games and still remembers the 'brutal riding and bullish physique of the Meares sisters'.

Her autobiography makes it abundantly clear how large Anna Meares loomed in Pendleton's mind.

Generally, in an autobiography of an athlete, you would expect to wade a few chapters in before encountering the career's major sporting rivalries. But how far into *Between the Lines* do you have to go to get to Meares? Page two. As early as that, Pendleton introduces her as 'my old rival, the Australian rider who so often tries to bully and intimidate me'.

How did we go from Stuttgart to that? From friend to foe? Or is it just that when two girls are headed in the same direction, towards being the best female sprinter the track world has ever seen, the clash is inevitable?

This is the story of two very different characters whose career paths seemed destined for a final, decisive showdown at Pendleton's home Olympics.

Immersed deeply in the psychology of this rivalry is the concept of femininity. Is it feminine to be brutal and bullish? Is it possible to be a world-class female athlete and yet retain your femininity?

Does success on the world stage require a young lady to bulk up until she resembles a man more than a woman? And what about the concept of the strong woman? Femininity does not necessarily equate to weakness, does it? Over a decade, both Meares and Pendleton would go about finding their own answers. And their answers would be reflected in their success and the way they handled a bike.

When first acquainted with international competition, at the European Championships in the Czech Republic in 2001, Pendleton was disconcerted. She did not like what she saw. She saw girls with mullet haircuts and big, muscular, powerful body-frames – the Russians in particular. Some riders would try to intimidate her, make her feel little, which she was by comparison. The Russian riders would even smack her on the bum in a patronising way, to let her know that she was small and not really in the right place. This was a world of alpha females and Pendleton never felt very alpha. She didn't appear to have the psyche or the figure of a sprinter.

Around British Cycling, she was aware of this too. She was petite and pretty and not remotely interested in morphing into the body type she was towered over by in the Czech Republic. So she would pitch up to training in mini skirts and sparkly sandals. Exactly what the likes of Chris Hoy and the other leading male riders in the group made of all this is irrelevant; what is not is Pendleton's own paranoia, her belief that they were all judging her as a misfit.

Yet as the years passed and Pendleton's medal collection grew, her looks became part of her tale.

She enjoyed being different; she did photo shoots for glamour mags, she posed naked on a bike. And she relished her position as a role model. Her message was simple: you can be good looking and feminine and still win bike races; the two are not mutually exclusive.

As she explained in her own inimitable way: 'I'm still a girl and I like wearing dresses and no one wants to look like a guy in drag, do they, when they put on a frock? For every big girl out there [competing against her in the velodrome], it's like an insult that they get beaten by some scrawny girly chick. Girls have looked at me as if to say: "How the hell did that beat me?"'

When growing up in Brisbane, Australia, a very different mindset was taking hold for Anna Meares.

She was never petite and she grew up acutely aware of that fact. Being an Aussie, hers was an outdoors life and trips to go swimming or to the beach made her self-conscious about her appearance; rather than dress down to bikinis or swimsuits, she would go the other way and cover up with shorts and T-shirts.

Yet as Meares grew successful on a bike and came to realise that she was commanding a growing army of followers, she started to take her position as a role model seriously, too.

'I slowly realised the effect I can have on people,' is how she explains it. 'I love being involved in sport because it shows kids a different stereotypical image of what it is to be a strong woman. It's not always about being skinny. It's about your presentation and your confidence and everyone is unique. It's accepting that you are different and being proud of the qualities that make you different. The women I compete with are strong, powerful women, who have curves, muscle and confidence. If that message is something I can give to kids, I'd be really pleased.

'I got teased a little bit when I was a kid because I had a big butt, but I put it to good use. It's difficult when you are young girl, and you see all the magazines and the beautiful girls in bikinis, and you just don't have that physical confidence. But as I have grown up, I've realised: I have a big butt , I don't have the model physiology and it doesn't bother me. It makes it hard to find jeans, though!'

Meares laughs as she says this. She is, indeed, very happy within her own skin. But the contrast with Pendleton is striking: two female world stars, two different messages, one saying that it is okay to be small and pretty, the other saying that it is okay if you are not. Yet not far from all this was the assertion, from Pendleton, that one thinks that it is okay to ride like a brute and the other does not.

This all came to a head in a single Keirin race at the World Championships in Bordeaux in 2006 when neither Pendleton nor either of the two Meares sisters qualified directly for the final and had to go through the repechage round, where two of six would go through. It didn't help, either, that Simona Krupeck-aite, the talented Lithuanian, was in the same race. This was a very classy field.

And as Pendleton would soon realise, it was also stacked against her. Two on one: a pair of Meares sisters in what Pendleton calls 'a brutal plan' and 'a calculated assault'. It was not very complicated, either. Anna's job, it seems, was to sacrifice her own ambitions for Kerrie by taking out Pendleton. Thus, when Pendleton mounted her first attack, Anna, in front of her, swung her wheel right, nearly knocking Pendleton from her bike and into the advertising boards.

The manoeuvre required some agile, high-speed bike-handling from Pendleton to stay upright, but it certainly succeeded in taking her out of the race, and it got Meares relegated, too. Pendleton was livid. Meares attempted to apologise, but Pendleton, in a cool, controlled fury, said: 'Don't talk to me.'

But that was really only the culmination. As she makes clear in *Between the Lines*, Pendleton had long been preoccupied with her Australian rival. At the

World Championships the previous year, in Los Angeles, Pendleton was rattled with self-doubt.

'I did not feel I deserved to be there,' she writes. 'A rider as unforgiving as Anna Meares would demolish me. How could I face her down when I felt so vulnerable?'

Los Angeles, however, was to be Pendleton's launchpad; it was there that she won her first sprint world title and she beat Meares in the semi-final in the process. Yet her description of that semi-final win also tells a story.

'I was in the World Championship final,' she writes. 'I had won, at the very least, a silver medal. But it mattered more to me that I had the sprinter's scalp of Anna Meares.'

* * *

What is it that drives a world-class athlete and then keeps on driving them? The psychology of Pendleton versus Meares is fascinating. Meares: comparatively balanced. Pendleton: an athlete so openly vulnerable who, at her lowest, would self-harm, cutting herself with nail scissors. Yet in one way they were closely twinned: they both grew up chasing a family member who was their better.

Pendleton chased her father. Meares chased elder sister Kerrie.

Max Pendleton, the father, was a national grass-track champion and a biking obsessive. Young Victoria grew up watching him win races and attempting to train with him on long cold rides on interminably long hills. She followed him on a bike because she found that this was the way to his heart. As a child, she never even contemplated the idea that she might be better than him.

Meares grew up in a competitive tussle with Kerrie. But Kerrie was not only older; she was naturally better. Kerrie was the kind of kid who won everything: area honours, junior national honours, headlines and attention. She was the one destined to go far. Anna was the not-so-good younger sister. At least, that is how she felt. She did not collect junior titles – she just worked bloody hard to finish towards the top of the pile. But it was the knowledge that she was not so naturally blessed that drove her forward. It drove her in everything – in school, in sports, even in competing with Kerrie for who would get to sit in the front seat of their parents' car.

And when she broke through into the elite, it required her to clamber past her sister, too. She acknowledges how hard that was, that her selection for the Athens and Beijing Olympics required her to trample all over her sister's dreams. Only one sister could go and Anna went to both. Kerrie eventually retired in 2010; two years on, the two sisters still hardly talk about their own rivalry.

'It's hard for both of us,' is how Anna explains it.

'It's hard for Kerrie to see that I am doing the things she wanted to do. We have a level of respect and understanding where we are both aware but we don't dabble in it too much.'

Yet Meares powered ever onwards. Of her and Pendleton, she won the first Olympic gold medal, in the 500-metre time trial in Athens in 2004, but after that event was scrapped from the Olympic programme, she found herself behind her rival in the two individual events that they would contest in London. Pendleton won Olympic gold in Beijing, beating Meares in the sprint final; at World Championship level, Pendleton would be undefeated champion every year from 2007 to 2010. Only thereafter did Meares catch her, and then, in 2011, overtake her. So 2012 would simply be a battle royal.

The fight would be waged on three battlegrounds: first, the World Cup event in London, at the new Olympic velodrome, then the World Championships in Melbourne, Australia, and then back again to London for the Olympics. From Pendleton's home turf to Meares's and back again, the heat turning up a notch every time.

In London the first time, they traded blows. Pendleton showed promising form, Meares then beat her 2-1 in their semi-final in the sprint, while in the Keirin they were both so busy watching each other that nether got on the podium.

That was an interesting start, though merely

an hors d'oeuvre. They arrived in Melbourne with Meares expected to deliver on home soil and with question marks over whether Pendleton was too far past her best. Melbourne was also where the rivalry was raised, by the media, to the level of soap-opera cat-spat, the two of them seemingly eagerly helping it on its way.

Meares said: 'You can't have a great friendship because there is so much riding on the line for those involved.' Pendleton then replied: 'I've heard her make some comments about how she dislikes me and I dislike her.' Even Meares's friend and sprint team partner, Kaarle McCulloch, got in on the act, saying: 'To be honest, I think Vicky's a little scared.' Often, too, there were reminders from Pendleton of Meares's tactics and her apparent record of rough-house riding.

That they would meet in the semi-final was a shame, albeit a kind of irrelevance. Their match-up here felt like the final and had the intensity of it, too – especially after the first race when the two clashed and Pendleton fell, hitting the deck at approximately 40mph, her skinsuit shredded so badly she sustained track burn from her hip to her shoulder.

At that stage, consensus had it that Pendleton was beaten, that for anyone to come back from that kind of a fall was a big ask of anyone. But Pendleton? Fragile of mind and confidence? No chance.

So it was inspiring simply to see her stepping

out to the track to contest round two. Then, when Meares was relegated for riding out of her lane, and they were tied one-all, it was clear that there was some exceedingly special racing unfolding before our eyes. The decider raised the standard even higher: they needed a photo finish to split them, and it was Pendleton, by an inch, who was the victor.

She then won her final and Meares won the bronze medal match, but that really did seem almost irrelevant. All that seemed to count was that Pendleton had beaten Meares.

But if anyone thought that Meares was some kind of dastardly rival, they only needed to hear her comments afterwards. She was distraught, fighting back tears of disappointment, and yet of Pendleton's crash, she said this: 'I saw it, I heard it, I felt it. That just goes to show Australia and the world that she can pick herself up and dust herself off – and she's a great champion for that.

'But I do feel very proud that I have a rival who, in the end, I have to work with to raise the bar of women's sprinting. We are two very strong, very powerful, very independent women and we are very proud of that.'

In Melbourne, Meares conducted herself with utter class. After the sprint, Pendleton's spirit was spent; she contested the Keirin but did not have it in her to make a fight of it. Meares, though, battled on. She won the Keirin and then just kept on

going. On the bill on the last day of the championships was the 500-metre time trial, which was not an
Olympic event, but the fact that Meares won that,
too, spoke volumes of her competitive spirit, heart
and soul.

But even that was not enough. As she said: 'The
big dance is in London in a few months' time.'

* * *

By the time Meares had arrived for the Games, the
pair's rivalry was pure tabloid fodder. Pendleton fed
the newspapers with some trademark barbs; indeed,
Pendleton was always their better provider.

But their apparent antipathy was such an
established theme in the build-up to the Games that
at a press conference hosted by Adidas, the first
question to Pendleton came from an Australian journalist, who asked: 'Anna Meares – is she a cow?' (The
answer, as it happens, was, 'Definitely not,' though
Pendleton was never going to say, 'Yes – she's a
complete bitch.')

It was also well known that Pendleton was retiring after these Games, that the pair would never race
each other again, that this was it: the final of finals,
the end of the road, the last shot at hegemony.

The first race was the Keirin, and it was all Pendleton's. The home girl, 'Queen Vic', came out faster
and stronger than ever, not remotely like someone

who might be past their best, pumped with confidence, too, and so quick that she felt happy to take on the race and ask the question: 'Can any of you match me?' And they couldn't. Not even Meares. In fact, especially not Meares. Meares didn't even make it onto the podium. The pendulum of power had swung completely.

It seemed at that stage that we knew the final answer to their rivalry – that Pendleton was indeed queen, the winner, the better. But this rivalry was epic because no one ever gave up, no one ever conceded defeat.

That race, Meares would say later, was the biggest let-down of her entire life. But that night, she sat with her coach, Gary West, in the food hall in the athletes' village and he wrote down a question for her on a napkin: 'What do you want to do?' And she wrote back the words: 'Keep doing what we know to do and keep on fighting.'

And so to the last fight of all. Meares was well prepared for this, meticulously so. Back at home, she and West had worked on a specific programme that they called Project Know Your Enemy.

The enemy was Pendleton and they trained every day with a male sprinter, Alex Bird, whose job was to be Pendleton while Meares learned how to beat him. This was like a boxer hiring a sparring partner to copy his opponent – and it was genius.

In the individual sprint, the good news was that

Pendleton and Meares did not meet in the semi-final; this time they would meet in the final or not at all.

And in race one, Project Know Your Enemy started to come good. Indeed, the tactics for this race were the culmination of an entire decade. Meares gave Pendleton the inside line and, coming off the banking into the back straight, appeared to dive-bomb her. She shot down off the bank straight at her.

Remember, here, that Pendleton's mind is full of images of rough-house riding and her brutish rival, because this is where Meares used that psychology entirely to her advantage. She did not ride a lady-like race, not at all; she rode exactly true to Pendleton's mental image. So when she flew down towards Pendleton, their elbows suddenly touching, Pendleton's response was to swing upwards to protect herself, and in that split-second, completely instinctive decision, Pendleton lost the race.

She would beat Meares to the finish but, in swinging out of her lane, she earned herself a disqualification. Meares's move was brilliant, and it had worked.

Was this good sportsmanship? Meares was unmoved by the question. 'This is a sport,' she said. 'We're not out there to have a cup of tea.'

Now 1-0 up and confident, the Australian had something for the second race, too. She knew that Pendleton was phenomenal at chasing, winning by coming off her opponent's wheel, so she wanted to test her by making her go ahead. Thus, after leading her out, Meares suddenly stopped. It is not unusual to halt on the pedals like this in a sprint, but it is as late into the race as Meares did it.

Pendleton, caught by surprise, had no alternative than to come past. It was that or fall off, and suddenly her own plans were in disarray. From that point, she led the race, but with little conviction, and Meares zipped by her comprehensively in the sprint to the line.

'I knew three weeks ago that I was going to do that,' Meares said. It was a plan that worked to perfection. The gold was hers.

And that is the end. Kind of. One-all. One gold each. The spoils shared. But it seemed they were both glad it was over. Neither had the appetite for any more. In Pendleton's case, not ever. But although they had scrapped stupendously for the week, the year, the decade, they also recognised their debt to one another.

Meares would never have been as great without Pendleton. And, likewise, Pendleton was elevated to greatness by her desire to beat Meares. Together, they lifted their sport.

In the context of track cycling, this was as good as Ali-Frazier, Ovett-Coe or Borg-McEnroe. This was as good as women's track sprinting had ever been. A golden era. Only at the end, when the fighting was done, did they realise how much they needed each other, and reflect on what they had done for each other.

In the London velodrome, when you await your medal ceremony, the medallists sit downstairs, out of sight, under the track. It was there that a kind of respectful truce was finally declared; they were down there waiting for a long time, around 20 minutes, and the subject of conversation was wedding dresses. They talked about Pendleton's forthcoming wedding, and Meares's wedding the previous year. They laughed together.

And there, you wondered the extent to which they really had disliked each other, or if they simply spent 10 years climbing on each other's shoulders to get even higher. For under the London velodrome track, sitting, waiting, the two great rivals became girls again, just like they had been in that bar in Stuttgart a decade before.

Owen Slot is the chief sports reporter for *The Times*. He has written five books, one of which he believes in the only children's book ever written on the subject of Keirin racing. Despite completing the 2007 Race Across America, he was never offered a professional contract as a rider.

8

If riding the Tour de France is considered an extraordinary feat, try riding the Tour, the Giro d'Italia and the Vuelta a España in the same season.

Lionel Birnie gets the inside line from Lotto-Belisol's Australian rider Adam Hansen on what it's really like to ride all three grand tours in a single summer.

THE GRAND SLAM

BY LIONEL BIRNIE

Adam Hansen sets his alarm every night and every morning he wakes well before it sounds. He sets it as insurance because very occasionally, when he's at home, he will oversleep and lunchtime will be approaching before he finally stirs. But when he is riding one of the grand tours, even when he is deep into the final week and his body is swaddled by fatigue, he finds he wakes naturally.

The grand tours, cycling's three-week events that push and pull at the boundaries of physical endurance and mental patience, have a rhythm and routine of their own.

It takes a special kind of temperament to thrive in such a gruelling environment. They are exhilarating yet at the same time mundane and survival requires an ability to submit to the grand tour's will, go with the flow and embrace that rhythm and routine.

Hansen, a 31-year-old Australian, has carved out a niche as a respected worker, or *domestique*, accepting long ago that, despite a talent that would make club cyclists gasp, his role in the professional sport is mostly to fetch, carry and support the stars.

But he did harbour an ambition of his own and in 2012 he achieved it by joining a small band of riders to complete the Giro d'Italia, Tour de France and Vuelta a España in the same season. Only 31 other riders have done that. They used to say that finishing the Tour de France made a rider a giant of the road. If that is the case, Hansen and the others must surely stand upon the shoulders of those giants.

Hansen rides for Lotto-Belisol, a Belgian team. Having come to Europe a decade ago, he rode for some small teams in Austria when dreams of starting one grand tour, let alone finishing three, felt a long way off. It wasn't until 2007 that he got a break, joining T-Mobile, and completing the Vuelta towards the end of that year. Having then experienced the Giro and the Tour, an idea began to form.

Most team managers would dismiss the notion of tackling such a heavy three-course menu as madness; needless, in fact, considering the number of riders the big teams have at their disposal.

Think of the numbers for a moment. That's nine weeks of intense racing in the space of just under four months. Combined, the Giro, Tour and Vuelta covered 10,300 kilometres in 63 days and Hansen spent more than 273 hours in the saddle.

The idea lurked at the back of his mind when he agreed his racing programme with the team's management. The Giro was confirmed at the start of the year, and once he had earned selection for the Tour he decided that he would do all three. 'I asked the management if I could do the Vuelta and when I saw the riders they put in that race I asked why I wasn't going,' he says. 'They thought I was joking but when they realised I wanted to do all three they were happy to let me. The grand tours are hard on the body and to see if I could handle all three in one year is something that has always puzzled me.'

Opting to ride the Vuelta could even be considered the preferable option when you consider the alternative. 'I knew the Vuelta would be full-on but I knew what I was letting myself in for,' he says. 'If I hadn't done the Vuelta, I might have been sent to 10 one-day races, all over Europe, so you're travelling much more, backwards and forwards from home.'

So it comes down to routine and rhythm again. A grand tour might be hard, but at least it's predictable, comfortable even. The demands are constant. Once a rider steps on the treadmill, it keeps moving until he reaches Milan, Paris or Madrid. Each rider is stuck in a loop, living his own personal Groundhog Day.

'It's exactly that,' says Hansen. 'You wake up in a hotel, you have the same breakfast with the same people, you pack your case, walk to the bus, sit in the same seat, listen to the same sports director, you put your numbers on and race – this is the only bit that's different – then you go to another hotel, have a massage from the same guy, eat dinner with the same group, share a room with the same guy. Mentally, being in a hotel so long, living out of a suitcase, that's the hard bit. I'm a pretty relaxed guy, I think I'm slow to get angry or annoyed, and I don't complain. You just have to let things go.'

* * *

The Giro started in Herning, Denmark, meaning a gruelling transfer early in the race and a long 12-day stretch between rest days. The riders may have grumbled but they have to take what's in front of them.

Hansen had a free role because Lotto did not have a rider to chase the pink jersey or a recognised sprinter. He played his cards a couple of times. As the peloton sped towards Fano at the end of stage five, he tried the impossible, to outrun the Sky train, but his effort was short-lived. Four days later, he tried again, with the same result, and then on stage 12 to Sestri Levante, he crashed hard.

As Hansen picked himself up, his legs buckled as they struggled to take his weight. He was convinced he'd broken a bone. He pressed his collarbone – it wasn't that, so he thought it was something deeper in his core. Because he was able to get back on his bike and could pedal, he chased the race to the finish.

'When you really hurt yourself in a race, you have two choices,' he says. 'You can jump in the car with the sports director and go to the finish, or you can ride and see if you recover a bit. If you get in the car, you get to the finish at the same time as if you'd ridden but your race is over, so it's a simple choice.'

Hansen's team-mate Lars Bak won the stage that day, while Hansen headed straight to the hospital for an x-ray, which turned out to be clear. After the Giro finished, he went for an MRI scan and as the results were assessed, the specialist said: 'Well, your sternum is in very good shape. It's broken in the bottom third but it's healing well. You must be in the second week of recovery now.'

The Giro is perplexingly schizophrenic. The atmosphere is laid back, yet frenetic. The fans are respectful but full of fiery passion. The stages can be long, the transfers even longer but the race has a more homely feel too, which Hansen says the riders appreciate.

'We sometimes have some really long days – 220 kilometres or 260 kilometres – sometimes even back to back,' he says. 'And there are no limits to what the organiser lays on for you. There's always some crazy uphill or dirt road you'd never ride your bike up. Sometimes there's snow on the side of the road. But the hotels are the nicest and the food is the best.'

Italy and Spain have not (yet) submitted to the rise of the faceless chain hotel, situated on a ring road or roundabout the way the French have. The menu and decor in one hotel is the same as in another branch 200 kilometres away so you never really know where you are. The Giro still uses family-run places that turn out great plates of pasta. Many of the teams take their own chef to the Tour de France but at the Giro and Vuelta they are in the hands of the kitchen staff. One of the mysteries of France is how a country with such a fine gastronomic reputation can have hotels that so often produce such bad food. 'It's terrible,' says Hansen, 'At school we were taught that France is famous for its great food and wine. On the Tour we don't get the best restaurants but I think the average is just not very good.'

Not that the riders are fussy. During a grand tour, their needs are basic, although there's one question everyone asks when they get to their hotel for the night. 'Is there internet? That's the most important thing,' says Hansen. 'The second question is whether it's free. That really changes the morale in the team. It means you can sit in bed, talk to your friends and family on Skype, keep up with the world.'

France is well plugged in but in rural Italy and Spain the information superhighway is still little more than a back road. Sometimes there isn't even a strong enough mobile phone signal to make a call, and that's when the grand tour experience can begin to feel isolating, particularly if there's a run of nights without a fast link to the outside world.

Everyone knows the Tour de France is the biggest race in the world. It's where the stress levels escalate, fans swarm round the riders and the journalists want their pound of flesh too. Sometimes it can get too much, Hansen says. 'You get people writing to you saying they went to school with you in grade two, or something, asking how the Tour's going.'

The racing is faster and less forgiving. Everyone has a job to do and nerves are fraught, particularly early on. Hansen's job was to help André Greipel in the sprints and then support Jurgen Van den Broeck, the team's hope for a high overall placing.

Greipel won three stages and Van den Broeck finished fourth overall, so the Tour can be considered a success. Van den Broeck would have been closer to the podium had he not punctured a few kilometres before the start of the Tour's first serious climb, La Planche des Belles Filles. Hansen was close by when it happened and paced his team-mate as he tried to regain contact, before the climb started to bite and he had no choice but to leave Van den Broeck and Lotto's other climber Jelle Vanendert to it.

Any thoughts of sneaking away in a break were banished – 'I was strictly told not to go in a breakaway, as I always had to be around the team leaders' – until the 18th stage from Blagnac to Brive-la-Gaillard, when Hansen went with an early escape and then hitched a ride with Alexandre Vinokourov, Luca Paolini and Nick Nuyens, who had launched a counter-attack in the closing kilometres. They didn't make it. Just as had happened in Fano, Italy, Sky shut it down and set Cavendish up for another win.

The rest of the time, Hansen was one of the ubiquitous yet almost invisible foot soldiers of the peloton. The viewers watch on television, looking out for the star riders, barely noticing the busy industry of the other 90 per cent. Setting the pace, shepherding the team leaders into position, chasing breaks, fetching water bottles and rain capes, a *domestique*'s work is never done.

* * *

'Your personal life goes on hold for three weeks,' says Hansen of the bubble that the professional riders occupy during grand tour season. 'You leave everything at home and life stops. You come home, the spider webs are throughout your house, the grass is well overdue a cut, the mail has piled up and, if you've forgotten, there's rotten food in the fridge.

'While you're away, you have zero time alone. You're with your team for almost four weeks. For me, that's hard. It can be relaxing because you don't have to think – everything is done for you. You're told what time to get up and what time to eat, and when the race is going well, even though it's hard work, it's great.

'A good room-mate is very important. I was with Greg Henderson at the Tour, who was good company. At the Vuelta I was with Vicente Reynes, who's a great guy and can be very funny but sometimes it's just a bit too much. Olivier Kaisen is about the best room-mate I've ever had. We shared at the Giro and he's much like me – quiet, relaxed, talks little. Don't get me wrong, I like to have a chat, but I need my down time. Olivier is very keen, professional.

'One team-mate from my last team would piss with the seat down and he wasn't a sharp shooter either. It's the little things that are difficult – the guy who wants the aircon running full on the whole time, or the guy who has the TV super loud late at night. I'm not perfect either – I'm not a big sleeper and sometimes I'm up late.'

* * *

Hansen counts the 2012 Vuelta a España as the hardest race he's ever done. The relentless climbing gave him the impression that the organisers were trying to make the riders look stupid.

'Some of the stages did become a joke – we're riding up there on compact chainsets and it looks easier on TV than it is. If you'd finished those stages three kilometres earlier you'd have had the same result, so what were they trying to do?

'I was hoping the Vuelta would get easier but I'd made my choice and I had to continue with it.'

Of the three, the Vuelta can be the scruffiest. One of the hotels was so bad the Lotto team checked in somewhere else instead. The soigneurs, having finished one lot of work, grabbed an hour's sleep before the riders' arrival heralded the start of a block of massaging, and awoke itching. The beds were infested with lice. Fortunately that is a rarity but when everything lines up to conspire against a rider – a crash, a bad hotel, a miserable dinner, no connection with the outside world – a grand tour can become a trial, a battle to survive.

A crash at the end of the first week almost put Hansen's grand slam in jeopardy but the x-rays showed his pelvis wasn't broken so although it was painful, he did what he always does and pushed on.

By the time the race arrived in Madrid, news of his feat had spread. He got plenty of pats on the back that afternoon and the scale of achievement began to dawn on him.

'People always ask, "Have you done the Tour?" Now I can say I've done all three of the big ones in the same year. Sometimes I wondered, "Why am I doing this?" but I am glad I did.'

* * *

After arriving in Madrid, Hansen headed home, which is in the Czech Republic, near the border with Slovakia. It's quiet, beautiful and about as far removed from the hub of European cycling as possible. That's deliberate. It means he can easily separate his home life from his professional life. Once a grand tour is ticked off, he escapes that world until it's time for his next assignment.

'Originally I moved here because of a girl and I enjoy living here. I spend 150 days a year with my cycling team-mates, which is plenty.'

Hansen doesn't strike you as an insular type. Focused, yes, but not to the exclusion of all else. He tries to take in everything he sees on the road but says the racing is too hard for it to be anything but a blur at times.

'A lot of riders could not point out on a map where they are,' he says. 'They couldn't tell you the name of the town they're in. They get on a bus that takes them to the door of the hotel. In the race they follow the arrows. That's not being disrespectful, it's just that we're not on holiday. I like to know where I am but do I think, "Let's research this place, find out about its history"? No.

'You get a sense of déjà-vu. You can be coming down some road and you think, "I've been here before," and I'm not talking about the Alps and Pyrenees and the places we go every year. Sometimes you get a bad sense of déjà-vu when you know what's coming up. Vicente is an experienced rider and he knows every single road in Spain, but for me, a foreigner, in a country where I don't speak the language, it doesn't matter too much where you are. If you do 10 years as a pro, 100 days of racing a year, that's a thousand different villages, towns and cities.'

When it's all over, Hansen says the riders tend to remember the very good days or the very bad. The rest merge into a whirr of chain noise and pedal strokes.

In all those 63 days of racing, which took him from Scandinavia to the ankle of Italy, from the Ardennes to the Ardèche and from one side of Spain to the other, and back again, Hansen says he never once came close to quitting.

'As you get older, and you have the experience, you know a bad day on the bike just means you will be at the back of the bunch. You just have to be a bit clever to make the best out of the worst situation. If you accept you're having a bad day in the mountains, you can find a group that is realistic for you – don't go with a group that's out of your league for that particular day.'

His worst day of the year comes readily to mind. 'Probably the stage towards the end of the Vuelta that Alberto Contador won, the day when he attacked and took the jersey. We'd done day after day of stupid steep climbs, all in little gears, and then it was suddenly much more undulating, hard and fast in bigger gears.

'It was so aggressive and so difficult. Everyone was scared they wouldn't be able to hold on when the race went fast, which ended up making the race fast because no one wants to be at the back, in danger of being left behind. There were so many guys in the *gruppetto* that day – probably 120. There were riders in there I'd never seen in the *gruppetto* before. And it was still hard. Up and down.'

Again, it comes back to the grand tour survival mantra. Routine and rhythm. After days in the mountains, the supposedly gentler terrain was, in fact, a shock to the tired legs. Don't upset the rhythm, don't mess with the routine.

Hansen began his season with the Australian Championships and Tour Down Under in January, and ended it at the Tour of Beijing in October. That's 10 months on the road, camaraderie and loneliness in equal measure.

'You can play with your mind so much,' he says. 'In cycling, you have a lot of time to think. You can spend a grand tour talking to yourself the whole way round. Often you have to think about something that's not related to the bike – stuff at home, my relationship, projects I'm working on – whatever it takes to speed up the time and make it a bit easier.'

So, would Hansen attempt the grand slam again?

'Maybe. We'll see next year.'

Lionel Birnie joined *Cycling Weekly* a week after the Festina affair in 1998. He covered his first Tour de France in 1999, then left the world of cycling in 2001, returning three years later. Comeback 2.0, they didn't call it. Today he writes for *The Sunday Times* and *Cycle Sport* and runs Peloton Publishing.

9

Richard Moore recalls his pursuit of the protagonist of his book, *In Search of Robert Millar*, and wonders how the Scottish climber might have fitted in at Team Sky today had Millar been born a generation later.

THE ORIGINAL INDIVIDUALIST

BY RICHARD MOORE

For various reasons, I am glad I wrote *In Search of Robert Millar* when I did. It was 2005 when I first had the idea, the inspiration being my admiration and my curiosity, the former for his achievements, the latter piqued by the burning questions: what had happened to him; where was he?

But that was the problem, too. It made the writing of his story difficult, if not impossible. I discussed it one evening with a journalist friend in a pub in Edinburgh, after he asked the question journalists always ask each other: 'Have you got a book in you?'

Millar's story of growing up in Glasgow and heading off to France and a remarkable career as one of the world's top cyclists was the one that came instantly to mind, but I explained the insurmountable obstacle: his disappearance. How could you write a book about somebody whose whereabouts are a mystery?

'Why not go "in search of"?' suggested my friend. And the penny dropped. So in fact it wasn't my idea at all, but my friend's.

For the next 18 months I researched and wrote, but here's the curious thing: I didn't really want to find him. Or rather, I didn't consider it necessary. That was the genius of the suggestion: the story would be about the search rather than the discovery; the 'discovery' would be somehow contained in the search. It would be this that would peel away the layers of Millar's complicated personality, perhaps offering up clues as to his whereabouts, or, even more intriguingly, perhaps not.

The book was published almost two years after that initial conversation, in June 2007. The timing was deliberate, to coincide with the Tour de France starting in London. It was to prove fortunate in other ways. And unfortunate, too, in a way that still causes regret for me, and no doubt worse for Robert Millar.

Why fortunate? Well, we can now see the 2007 Tour as a pivotal moment for British cycling. When I pitched a biography of Millar, the sub-title wrote itself: it would be the story of Britain's greatest-ever Tour de France cyclist. There was no argument with that. It was all very simple in those days. Tom Simpson was the greatest one-day rider; Millar the greatest stage racer. No need for any further discussion. Move along.

And yet, two years later, came another book, *Boy Racer* by Mark Cavendish. A quote appeared on the jacket: 'Britain's best-ever Tour de France cyclist.' It might have been a weak claim at the time, though a stronger case could perhaps have been made a year or so later. And then, in 2012, it all changed again. But we'll return to that.

Back to 2007. The London *Grand Départ*, watched by millions in London and on the road to Canterbury, acted to galvanise the sport in Britain. Less than a week later, Dave Brailsford was telling a few journalists in Bourg-en-Bresse how inspired he had been by what he'd seen in London, and about his ambition to set up a British team, and ultimately to win the Tour with a British rider. Though that seemed highly unlikely, things were undoubtedly about to get interesting.

But at the time, despite the crowds in London and Kent, and a vaguer sense that several young British riders might go on to achieve great things, there was still only Robert Millar.

As if to underline his status, and to honour him, his namesake and fellow Scot, David Millar, attacked on the stage from London to Canterbury to claim the polka-dot jersey – the jersey that symbolises Robert's greatest achievement: his king of the mountains title (and fourth overall placing) at the 1984 Tour. (He remains the only English speaker ever to wear the polka-dots into Paris.)

Then, two years later, with Brailsford's dream project about to be realised, Bradley Wiggins matched the elder Millar's highest placing, finishing a remarkable fourth (though with Lance Armstrong stripped by the US Anti-Doping Agency of all his results from 1998, Wiggins should officially inherit Armstrong's third-place, and thus belatedly become the first British rider to finish on the podium. Although he would eventually do that, anyway. But this is getting confusing.)

Wiggins's performance in 2009 brought Robert back from the dead, so to speak, though I think a strong case could still have been made for him as our greatest-ever grand tour rider: two second-place finishes at the Vuelta a España and second at the Giro d'Italia, as well as his three mountain stage wins at the Tour, and his fourth and ninth overall finishes, make up a pretty impressive *palmarès*.

Why was the book's timing unfortunate? Well, this also links, in a way, to the changes we have witnessed over the past five years. The Tour coming to London in 2007 opened a small window of opportunity, which would slam shut again as soon as the race returned to France.

It meant that, for a couple of days, the nation's media would be interested in cycling and the Tour. And that meant potential interest in the story of Britain's greatest-ever Tour rider. Thus it was a good time to publish a book about him.

But on the morning of the *Grand Départ*, as I awoke at a friend's house, and prepared, with a sense of excitement and novelty, to go and report on the Tour de France in London, my phone bleeped with a text message: 'Have you seen the *Daily Mail*? They've got a story about Robert Millar.'

I felt queasy. Writing a book like the one I'd tried to write, in which I tried to satisfy the reader's curiosity while simultaneously respecting Millar's very obvious desire for privacy, had felt at times like tight-rope walking. There had been speculation about Millar, including a story in a Scottish tabloid in 2000 alleging that he was having a sex change. It was a rumour I could hardly ignore, yet neither did I want to fan the flames of innuendo. It proved a difficult balancing act, but I was happy that the final part of the book comprised a series of emails between Robert and me. It meant he had the final word – that was satisfying.

I suspected, however, that the *Daily Mail* would not have – how shall I put this? – come at the story from the same angle. And so it proved. If I remember correctly, the story was on page seven: a position of prominence. I understood that it would not have been so prominent – indeed, would probably not have been written at all – had the Tour not been starting in London that day; and had I not written my book. (I was later told, by a *Daily Mail* journalist, that a reader had contacted the paper after a review of the book appeared on the sports pages; the reader claimed to be a neighbour of Millar, and tipped them off as to his whereabouts.)

The story ticked all the tabloid boxes: it purported

to be sensational, it was unsympathetic and cruel, it involved a terrible invasion of someone's privacy, and there was clearly no 'public interest' justification. It was hit-and-run journalism, a bit like a terrorist attack: catastrophic for the victim, and of no value whatsoever to anyone else.

I certainly don't regret writing the book. I think most readers understood what I was trying to do, and ended up with greater respect for Millar's achievements, and for his singular talent and approach, his eccentricities and foibles.

There is another question now, though – one that has arisen in the last five years, and intensified over the past 12 months.

It concerns how Millar might have fared in the new era of British cycling and in the Brailsford-managed Team Sky. It is tempting to dismiss any idea that a maverick like Millar could have fitted in, far less thrived, in such a regimented set-up, where every watt is logged, every ounce is weighed and effort calculated.

A while ago I asked another singular, and Scottish, individual, Graeme Obree, how he thought he'd have got on in such a system.

'Actually, I would have done terribly badly,' said Obree, and proceeded to explain that, as 'a privateer', he would be denied opportunities unless he conformed. And his character meant he wouldn't have been able to conform.

On first consideration, we might think the same of Millar. The argument would go that he 'did his own thing' by going to France to pursue his ambitions, which is often cited as evidence that he was a loner, a rebel, too independent to fit into any system. 'Individualist' is the term he liked to use.

Yet what it overlooks is that Millar, unlike Obree, did fit into a system: the continental professional cycling system. How else would he have sustained such a long (15-year) career as a professional, and why else would he have ridden for some of the world's top teams?

Millar was ambitious but also smart, and he figured out the best – at the time, only – route to a career as a professional on the continent (a route Obree could avoid, to a greater degree, because his ambitions lay on the track rather than the road). It was why he went off and 'did his own thing' in France, with a commitment that necessitated consciously cutting ties with old friends in Glasgow.

'I think he realised that, when he went to France, he didn't want to be missing his pals,' as one former friend told me. 'He didn't want anything to come back for, or it would have been too easy to pack it in and come home.'

Everything he did was designed to make life tolerable in France, where he knew he needed to be to fulfil his ambition. Before leaving, he began French lessons with one of his mentors, the late

Arthur Campbell. Millar had hardly bothered with school, rarely turned up for work – when he did, he spent as much time as possible sleeping in a store room – yet, in Campbell's weekly classes and with the homework he was assigned, he was a model pupil. This owed nothing to his interest in the language. 'Oh no, oh no,' laughed Campbell. 'It all came from his ambition to be a cyclist. It wasn't that he wanted to speak French!'

Had Millar been starting out now, he could have taken a different route. He might have decided that British Cycling and Team Sky could provide the optimum pathway to a career as a professional. He may have embraced this system and blossomed. His other old mentor and coach, Billy Bilsland, claims he would have won the Tour.

It is an impossible question. Millar in Team Sky kit? How would he have got on with Brailsford? He briefly worked under his predecessor, Peter Keen, as British road coach in 1997.

But Keen, from a sports science and coaching background, wanted to focus exclusively on track racing, didn't think Millar had strong management skills, and sacked him.

Millar was damning of the British Cycling approach – still focused mainly on track racing – when we exchanged emails in late 2006. He wrote: 'There's no creativity, it's all numbers and figures, which is great in a fixed environment like track racing... i.e. If you have this number of watts you'll go this fast and we'll know you can reach this level of competition. It's like painting by numbers, fill in the boxes and you'll complete the picture... Woohoooooo, isn't that clever? Trouble is, road racing isn't that controllable and if Picasso turned up for a job at the BCF [British Cycling Federation] paint school they'd tell him he was barking up the wrong tree.'

Yet, with glorious perversity, Millar himself was an innovator and something of a sports-science pioneer (even if the discipline was hardly recognised back then). He was certainly open to new ideas, although, rather than having these imposed upon him, he seemed to come up with many of them himself, mainly through reading books.

With regard to diet, he was enlightened, as Stephen Roche noted: 'Robert would come to the dinner table with these little bags of nuts, oils, raisins, hazelnuts... Regarding nutrition, diet, training, Robert was way ahead of his time. He would know how many calories he'd had that day; he knew everything. And you look over at the dinner table on a race now and all the French riders have these little bags...'

'Robert was the first guy to train with ankle weights on,' said Pascal Simon, a team-mate at Peugeot and neighbour in Troyes, where Millar lived. 'In fact, he was the only guy.'

Had power meters been available in the 1980s, Millar would surely have used one. He might not have been wedded to it, but he would have used it, and used it smartly.

At the 2012 Tour, as Wiggins rode to victory – a victory that owed rather more to 'numbers and figures' than to creativity, it must be said – another rider emerged who seemed more reminiscent of Millar. Chris Froome, on his way to second place overall, was a climber, like Millar, and he, too, was a bit different: not a product of the British Cycling system, like Wiggins, but quirky, erratic, a bit of an 'individualist'.

David Millar summed up the differences between Wiggins and Froome: 'Brad's your archetypal athlete, a class-A athlete who does everything in an incredibly detailed way; he's mechanical, very engaged and professional. Whereas Froome is a bit looser; he's a maverick, he comes from a different background. He's very much a self-made man. Brad is manufactured. Don't get me wrong, Brad has done it himself, but he's also the product of a system.'

As well as Froome, another British rider was beginning to earn comparisons to Robert Millar in 2012. Jonathan Tiernan-Locke, the first home winner of the Tour of Britain since Millar in 1989, will join Team Sky in 2013, and he comes with a reputation for also being a bit different, a left-field player.

They are a similar size (Tiernan-Locke, at 63 kilograms, is slightly heavier than Millar was), and climbing is their main weapon, but Tiernan-Locke has even more in common with Millar than you first realise. When he was 18, he, like Millar, went to France to pursue his dream of turning professional (it was 2003, and France was still the best option, with the British academy, which produced Cavendish, not opening its doors until 2005).

Tiernan-Locke went to the city in which Millar had lived: Troyes, joining the UV Aube club and coming into contact with Millar's old mentor, and the man at the centre of the Troyes cycling scene, Jack Andre.

While in France, Tiernan-Locke fell ill and his chance seemed to be lost. He returned home and went to university, then slowly recovered his health, returned to racing, and worked his way back through the ranks through British domestic teams.

Despite his singular focus, there was always more to Millar than just cycling. He had a hinterland. And so it is with Tiernan-Locke.

'I'm definitely appreciative of the fact I've done other things,' he said at the Tour of Britain. 'I've got a load of friends who aren't cyclists, that haven't just lived always in that bubble.'

The question of how someone like him, who has done his own thing, will fit into the Sky set-up has occurred to him, he admitted.

'But I'm not a maverick like Jez [Jeremy Hunt], say, and even he's integrated into that set-up. I'm quite open. In all areas of my life, I'm open to new ways of doing things. Plus, you can't ignore what they've done with the guys who've gone there. Pretty much everyone who has gone there has got better. I don't know someone who's gone and their performance has gone down. They've either prolonged their careers or they've had their best results there.'

It is possible that in 2013 and 2014, by watching Tiernan-Locke's progress, we will get an idea of how Millar might have got on at Team Sky. Brailsford wants Tiernan-Locke to lose five kilograms – so he will be more Millar's build – and believes that, as well as excelling on the shorter, punchier climbs, there is no reason why he can't also ride with the best in the high mountains.

It will be interesting. But will there ever be a more fascinating, compelling and original figure in British cycling than Robert Millar?

I'll finish with an anecdote that didn't make it into the book, because I only heard it afterwards. It ties into a concern I had at the outset: that I would do my research and speak to his old acquaintances and discover that, although I had admired him as a kid, I didn't actually like him as an adult. I think I would have found that book hard to write, but I needn't have worried. I did like Millar – and so, it seemed, did those few who felt they knew him best.

Although he could come across as prickly and rude, it seemed to me that Millar had (has) a good heart. And some further evidence for this came in an email I received after the book came out. It was from a reader, who recalled what was apparently a fairly routine incident – Millar being rude to fans before a race. The race was the Kellogg's Tour of Britain, before a stage start in Chester, and Millar was spotted by the teenager and his older brother. Both were fanatical Millar supporters.

'He was walking with a colleague an hour or so before the race and we asked for a photo.' Millar's response was curt. The fans were duly hurt. And they wrote about his 'sulky attitude' to *Cycling Weekly*, which published the letter.

'Two weeks later a French postal package arrived at the house, with a hand-written letter from Robert, apologising for his temper, explaining he was going through a lot of contract emotions... He had read *Cycling Weekly* and asked them for our address to make amends. Included in his package was one of his tops from the race, a pair of Z-Peugeot shorts, a signed photograph and a Z-Peugeot headband. Needless to say [this] restored his popularity with us.'

Richard Moore is a former racing cyclist and is now a journalist and author whose first book, *In Search of Robert Millar* (HarperSport), won Best Biography at the 2008 British Sports Book Awards. He is also the author of *Heroes, Villains & Velodromes*, *Slaying the Badger* and *Sky's the Limit*.

10

Ellis Bacon considers a phenomenon he's not even sure really exists: the role of luck in the professional peloton.

THE BEST OF LUCK

BY ELLIS BACON

I'd been to Châteauroux before, but only truly recognised the place from three years earlier once I stepped inside the local gym hall being used as the press room.

To be honest, I would have been deliriously happy to have stepped into a broom cupboard. Anywhere, really, as long as I was safe and in one piece.

I'd been lucky enough to be invited to 'enjoy' a ride on the back of a press motorbike during stage seven of the 2011 Tour de France – a rare opportunity to ride in and around the pro peloton on a leg of the world's biggest bike race. Years before, I'd turned down the invitation – I made up some excuse or other; really I was just scared – but had regretted it ever since. When the offer came again, I decided that I had to take advantage of it.

At the start of that seventh stage, on the outskirts of Le Mans, I felt woefully under-prepared, dressed as I was in jeans – my only alternative was shorts – and one of those paper-thin rain jackets that sticks to you at the faintest hint of any moisture.

While waiting for the call to tell me where to meet my motorbike driver, the heavens opened, and I had to seek shelter under the Euskaltel-Euskadi team bus's awning, where Basque mechanics were making last-minute tweaks to their riders' bikes.

Soon, I was making my way through the crowds to meet Bruno Thibout – an amiable former pro who'd ridden for teams such as Castorama, Motorola and Cofidis. He was now working for the Tour organisation, ferrying scaredy-cat journalists around France on a green Kawasaki.

The rain had stopped, too, but the pillion seat had sucked it all up, and my bum was soggy as soon as I sat down.

'Just let me know if you want to go slower or anything,' Bruno cheerfully told me before we set off, but I didn't really hear him say it at the time. It only came back to me a few hours later, once we had bolted from the peloton to head to the finish at Châteauroux, with around 40 kilometres left of the stage to go. And I mean bolted. On closed roads, we must have been doing at least a billion miles an hour. I've quite possibly never been so scared in my life.

With around 10 kilometres to go – and with very vivid visions in my head of a French holidaymaker stepping out into the road in front of us without looking, knowing that the riders weren't due for another half an hour – I had to give in. I gingerly tapped Bruno on the shoulder and, in the least wavering voice I could muster, asked whether we might be able to go *un peu plus lent* after skipping virtually sideways through another roundabout.

I didn't doubt for a second that he knew exactly what he was doing; I was simply petrified at the thought of skidding along the tarmac for about a kilometre on my wet backside.

Once we arrived safely in Châteauroux, we shook hands, and Bruno grinned and assured me that he had always been in complete control. I felt better in every way: better because he'd reassured me, better because I suddenly felt that I probably wasn't the first journalist he'd had to reassure that week, and better because I was off that huge green Kawasaki death machine.

So as I stumbled towards the press room to catch the end of the stage on the television, a vague feeling of familiarity about the place also nagging at my brain, I thought about how lucky I was. Lucky to have had an opportunity like that, to literally go inside the peloton and see up close the kind of unbelievable bike handling that goes on, and that we take for granted so often. Yes, I was lucky, I thought. Lucky to be alive, perhaps, too, and lucky that I hadn't told my wife what I was doing until my feet were back firmly – or firmly-ish – on terra firma.

But at what must have been the very moment Bruno and I had left the race behind to speed to the finish, 40 kilometres back up the road, Bradley

Wiggins was doing exactly what I had hoped to avoid: writhing around in agony at the side of the road after a crash in the bunch.

The result? A broken collarbone, which meant that he was out of the race – months of specific Tour training down the pan, all thanks to a touch of wheels.

Cavendish, then riding for HTC-Highroad, won his 17th Tour stage there in Châteauroux – the same town where I'd seen him win his first in 2008. Wiggins, meanwhile, was on the next plane home, keen to recover and refocus on the Vuelta a España and the World Championships.

The British were coming – rather, in 2011 they were well on their way – but on that 'lucky' seventh stage, the chasm between one, Cavendish, and the other, Wiggins, was a big one. The former couldn't have been happier, but said what he was supposed to in the post-stage press conference about hoping Wiggins was okay, while the latter's hopes of a Tour victory were left on the tarmac on the road from Le Mans to Châteauroux as he gingerly headed home.

* * *

A year later, the pair's roles – or fortunes – had reversed somewhat. Cavendish, the world champion, had joined Wiggins at Sky, and while 'The Manx Missile' streaked to three stage victories at the 2012

Tour, he clearly wasn't happy with playing second fiddle on a team with only one thing on its mind: overall Tour victory.

Wiggins, meanwhile, was almost glowing: basking in the confidence that intense, focused training, a win overall at Paris-Nice, victory at the Tour of Romandy and first place at the Critérium du Dauphiné must give you heading into your season's main objective. But he also lit up in my eyes as untouchable by the bad-luck gods. From the moment he took the yellow jersey on stage seven (ironically enough), for me there was absolutely no way he was going to lose it – especially not through another crash anyway.

How did I know this? Was it not obvious? He'd crashed the year before, and so this time he was sure to be okay.

Do I honestly believe what I'm writing, though? Of course I don't. In all walks of life, some people just get all the luck; others get none at all. The idea of there being a set amount of good luck and bad luck, in equal measures – 'You win some, you lose some' – just simply isn't true.

But in professional cycling, and at the Tour de France especially, it certainly appears to be the case more often than not. There was just no way Bradley Wiggins was going to crash out while in yellow. Seriously – I knew. I just knew.

Some would say – lucky people, usually – that you make your own luck – i.e. that luck isn't really luck at all, but intense, boring, plain-old-fashioned hard work that gets you something and somewhere. There are all those books these days proclaiming that it's X-thousand hours of practice that creates the best golfer or tennis player. Or cyclist? Of course. Wiggins, for one, knows that that's what won him the 2012 Tour.

Let's, for once, push the spectre of doping to one side for a few pages and accept that the long hours of training that pro riders do helps finesse speed and bike-handling. Practise makes perfect, and there can be little doubt that these pros are the best of the best: the fastest and the strongest, yes, but also the most skilled bike handlers who can get themselves out of a fix with a flick of the wrist or a twist of the lumbar. Just as I'd seen in the middle of the bunch while I'd been on the back of the scary motorbike. Only very rarely – especially when you consider just how many hours they spend on their bikes – do pro riders crash.

But luck, as a concept, can be viewed in a variety of ways, from a variety of angles. Many French fans view Raymond Poulidor as unlucky for having finished second overall at the Tour on three occasions, and third a whopping five times, without ever winning it. Is that really so unlucky, though? Most people would give their right arm to be able to say they'd finished on the Tour podium just once.

However, that isn't really the kind of luck I'm

thinking of here. What I'm talking about is the more cryptic, surely-doesn't-exist luck. Perhaps it borders on karma, or something more psychological. Either way, in cycling's storied history there are countless examples of hard-luck stories, yet strangely they are almost all tempered by something good happening before or after to the protagonist, too. Care for any examples? There are loads of them.

Spain's Pedro Delgado easily won the 1988 Tour, despite having tested positive along the way for the diuretic probenecid – a product that, although banned by the International Olympic Committee, was not at that point on the UCI banned list, and so Delgado escaped punishment. What a stroke of luck. But then the following year he missed his start time for the prologue time trial and was already almost three minutes down on his rivals before the race had even properly begun.

The winner of that 1989 Tour, Greg LeMond, had also won in 1986. But in a truly extraordinary piece of bad luck in the interim, he was accidentally shot by his brother-in-law while out hunting in California in April 1987. So it was only obvious that the stars would align once more to allow him to take the '89 Tour victory after such terrible luck, wasn't it?

Going back a little further again, French rider Eugène Christophe has to go down as one of the unluckiest riders in Tour history. That's right – he's the one whose forks broke on the descent of the Col du Tourmalet in 1913, forcing him to run the rest of the way down and find a blacksmith in the town of Sainte-Marie-de-Campan. A friendly 'smithy' allowed Christophe to use his workshop, but as the black-smith's assistant had helped the rider fix his bike by operating the bellows, Christophe was disqualified.

After surviving the First World War – a feat of luck in itself – Christophe went into the 1919 Tour as one of the favourites. On stage 11, three quarters of the way through the race, and having led overall for six stages, Christophe was handed the honour of being the first rider to wear the yellow jersey, intro-duced that morning at the start in Grenoble. Chris-tophe held it for four more days – and then his forks broke again on the penultimate stage, and Belgium's Firmin Lambot took ownership of the maillot jaune and kept it the next day to the finish at the Parc des Princes in Paris.

Swings and roundabouts: Christophe took the good with the bad.

And, for all that we perhaps shouldn't talk about him, what about Lance Armstrong? He enjoyed a remarkable run of good luck as a rider, followed later by the bad.

Armstrong was always deemed one of the luckier riders in the peloton, seemingly blessed with either the ability or the luck to avoid crashing too often.

Crashing while in yellow – or having your forks break, like Christophe – must be one of the

unluckiest fates to befall a pro. But someone, somewhere, was shining down on a yellow-clad Armstrong
when he was forced to plunge through a field on stage
nine of the 2003 Tour to avoid rival Joseba Beloki's
crash on the descent of the Côte de la Rochette into
Gap. Even if his Tour victory that year was achieved
fraudulently, that off-road escapade must nevertheless go down as one of the most extraordinary feats
in the race's history.

Armstrong's comeback, starting in 2009 – after
having retired following the 2005 Tour – was less
lucky, however. Then, like now, his luck really did
seem to have run out.

In his and Elizabeth Kreutz's photography
book, *Comeback 2.0: Up Close and Personal*, Armstrong
reveals that a friend of his gave him a good-luck
charm before the start of every Tour. But, after
retirement, the two lost touch, so Armstrong was
thrilled when the friend found him at the start of the
2009 Tour in Monaco and gave him a small gold fish
pendant 'that he'd had blessed by an Italian priest'.

It didn't seem to work. First Armstrong missed
out on wearing the yellow jersey again by just two
tenths of a second on the stage four team time trial,
before going on to finish third overall. Then, on one
stage of the 2010 Tour the following year, he seemed
to spend more time on the ground than on his bike.
On stage eight, having got caught up in, but managing to avoid, a huge crash in the peloton early on, on

a roundabout at the bottom of the Col de la Ramaz Armstrong clipped his pedal on the curb on his way round and crashed heavily.

He gave up after that, despite his RadioShack team-mates' efforts to shepherd him over the stage's remaining climbs. Nearing the top of the third-category climb of Les Gets, he went down again in a tangle of bikes and bodies.

As Armstrong stood with his hands on his hips, waiting for Saxo Bank rider Chris Anker Sørensen to pull his bike free from Armstrong's, you could al-most hear the American telling himself that this was not to be his Tour, and that this was probably the end of the road. In any case, it's my last impression of Armstrong the rider.

No, 'Comeback 2.0' was not a happy, nor lucky, one. It was almost as though he'd had his fair share of luck as a rider. But yes, enough about Armstrong. He may be a prime example of a rider who has expe-rienced the highs and lows of luck, but it's also very easy to argue that all those stories were simply the product of a sham.

Jonathan Vaughters – a former Armstrong team-mate – on the other hand is now at the vanguard of the anti-doping push in professional cycling, and he deserves every success. Especially after such a torrid time at the hands of the Tour de France gods as a rider. In four attempts, he never managed to finish the Tour – three times forced out by crashes, and once by a wasp. That sting, suffered on a training ride on the second rest day of the 2001 Tour, which caused his face to blow up like a balloon, could have been resolved by a shot of cortisone. Alas, UCI rules didn't permit it, and he had to quit – an unlucky victim at the arse-end of an insect.

* * *

Few pro riders appear to believe in being able to deflect bad luck. There are a few Saint Christopher chains knocking about, often having been given as gifts by loved ones, but otherwise riders just accept what the road gives them.

But one rider – one of Vaughters's charges at Garmin-Sharp, in fact – carries a small piece of wood with him on his bike so that he's able to 'knock on wood' in the hopes he'll come home safely from each race or training ride.

German pro Andreas Klier's idea for the My-Knoaky came from the day in April 2011 that he narrowly avoided being hit by a car when out training, and decided that being able to tap a small piece of oak that was attached to his frame might help to keep ill fortune at bay.

They're available to buy, too, with the proceeds going to tree-planting charity Plant for the Planet, which helps to ensure that millions of people around the world will be able to continue to ward off bad luck by 'touching wood', on their bikes or otherwise, long into the future.

Whether Team Sky's Alex Dowsett owns a My-Knoaky, I don't know, but he is somewhat of a believer when it comes to luck. At least, he used to be.

A team-mate to both Cavendish and Wiggins during the 2012 season, Dowsett has haemophilia, which means that a serious crash could, for him, be very serious indeed. Does he take fewer risks when he races as a result?

'The luck side of things is something I have in the back of my mind,' he says. 'I feel I've been very lucky my whole life being able to do what I've done with a condition that should have rendered me mildly disabled, plus so far in my cycling career I've been able to bounce reasonably well. I figured my bad luck this year [Dowsett broke his elbow at the 2012 Three Days of West Flanders] was payback for the luck I have had so far.'

But Dowsett admits that most of what happens is outside of his control, and so he wears a necklace stamped with his medical details in case of a bad accident when racing or training.

His biggest supporters – his family – have helped him carve a career out of the sport he loves despite his haemophilia, but his mum's also had to suffer the stress of watching her son in other ways.

'My mum is quite superstitious at the best of times and after coming to a few races where I didn't do so well – one being the British Junior National Road Race Championships one year, where I started as one of the favourites, yet wound up fourth – she decided that enough was enough.'

Dowsett's mum thought that she was bringing bad luck to his races, and stopped attending them.

'But Dad and I thought that this was a little silly,' continues Dowsett, and they encouraged her along to a few races in 2011. 'She came to only three races all year: the National Time Trial Championships, the London Nocturne and the final stage of the Tour du Poitou Charentes.'

Dowsett won them all, and the 'curse' was broken. If there had ever really been one in the first place.

'Now if I do badly, we, as a family, generally accept that it's probably down to me,' Dowsett grins.

Ellis Bacon is a British cycling writer and journalist who has covered nine Tours de France. He was deputy editor at *procycling* magazine for seven years before moving across to 'the enemy', *Cycle Sport*, in 2010. In 2012, he translated Bjarne Riis's autobiography *Riis: Stages of Light and Dark* (VSP) into English from Danish and authored *World's Ultimate Cycling Races* (Collins). He has more book projects in the pipeline, and still writes for various magazines, but has recently moved to California, which he knows means that he's pretty lucky. He hopes Greg LeMond's brother-in-law doesn't hunt there any more, though.

11

After a generation away from the world of cycling journalism, **Kenny Pryde** returned in spring 2012 to find a dramatically altered landscape.

Where once talk of doping was strictly taboo, he came back to find it was, at times, the only topic of conversation.

And while he recognises the refreshing openness, he wonders whether such a single-minded agenda is actually a good thing.

ANOTHER WORLD?

BY KENNY PRYDE

After a 14-year absence from cycling journalism, I made my 'comeback' at the 2012 edition of Flèche Wallonne, curious to rediscover a sport I've spent my adult life following. I had, obviously, been keeping an eye on the sport throughout, but from a safe distance. Actually, my timing was impeccable, both in terms of exit and re-entry.

The timing of my departure was lucky, as I left cycling for another branch of two-wheeled showbiz a couple of months before the contents of Willy Voet's Fiat Marea blew everything up back in July 1998. I surveyed the Festina affair fallout from the sidelines, saddened at the names who tumbled out of Voet's notebooks.

To tell the truth, I was glad that I didn't have to deal with it. Picking through the bones of relationships with 'my' rider contacts, like a bloke who has just discovered his wife has been cheating on him for years, would have been a wounder.

I read Voet's book, *Massacre à la Chaîne* and the one written by David Walsh and Pierre Ballester,

LA Confidentiel, with a combination of sadness and an almost complete lack of surprise.

When Brian Holm disgustedly noted (when riding for Tulip in 1992) that the idea that the ongoing Italian *risorgimento* in cycling 'is all about pasta and pulse monitors is just bullshit', there was a clue right there. Or when, in 1994, the Australian rider Phil Anderson, then at Motorola, told me that Michele Ferrari 'is just a chemist', he was onto something.

In the light of the Festina affair, I realised that in 1996, when Jean-Cyril Robin of Festina told me, apropos of doping, that the Italians were taking the piss, what he actually meant was that they were over-doing it, not simply just doing it. There were hints being dropped about what was taking place. But in the early 1990s, the topic of doping was still taboo and the EPO and blood manipulation tide had yet to overwhelm us all.

(As an aside, if a timid young journalist was registering concern from credible elements of the pro peloton, what the hell were the UCI, team managers and race organisers hearing? Were there no alarm bells ringing in those corridors of power in the early 1990s?)

It's only ever with a bit of hindsight and perspective that pieces fall into place. Back then, in the mid 1990s, those interchanges were about as far as anyone would go to discussing doping in the sport, and even then it was a quick way of pissing off riders whose co-operation you needed for information. Journalists were fishing, sifting rumours and listening to third-hand stories, and there wasn't much to go on.

Back then we were passing around faxes and photocopies of barely understood articles in haematology journals. Hell, back then the UCI hadn't even worked out that a haematocrit limit would be a good idea, and a dope-control test for EPO was still half a decade away.

So, 14 years on, in April 2012, I found myself in the press room of the Flèche Wallonne and back in the heart of a sport and a race I love.

Brian Holm is now *directeur sportif* at Omega Pharma, and Jean-Cyril Robin is driving an ASO car at the Tour de France, while Phil Anderson is a media pundit in Australia. And of course Dr Michele Ferrari is still a troubling figure in cycling. The UCI even has a test for human growth hormone now. The names of journalists staring at laptop screens in the press room have changed little – though they're older, greyer, heavier and have less hair (like me, funnily enough).

And we can all talk about doping now. In fact, as 2012 rolled on, from spring to autumn, it felt like the only story in town.

The fallout from Food and Drug Administration (FDA) investigator Jeff Novitzky's aborted investigation, the US Anti-Doping Agency (USADA) case against Lance Armstrong and the publication of

Tyler Hamilton's book, *The Secret Race*, meant doping was impossible to avoid for most of 2012, a backdrop against which the season played out.

On April 18, Joaquim 'Purito' Rodriguez sprinted clear of a select group at the steepest corner of the Mur de Huy to win the Flèche Wallonne and, after the podium flowers 'n' kisses were over, the Katusha rider sat down for his media grilling.

Unluckily for Rodriguez, his team-mate Denis Galimzyanov had tested positive for EPO the week before, following an out-of-competition test. Worse, you might say, throughout his career Rodriguez had ridden for a series of teams that had been implicated in doping scandals, from ONCE to Saunier Duval, via Caisse d'Epargne. And of course he was Spanish, which, for many observers, is already a sign of irredeemable moral turpitude.

In the small huddle of the press conference, the inevitable doping question was fired in by a Francophone Belgian journalist: 'So, er, what about your doped team-mate? You can understand why some people might have doubts about you, right? What's your position?'

'I'm pleased he was caught. It shows we are catching the cheats and we should be pleased,' stated Rodriguez, cornered behind a table, speaking through a translator.

And that's it really. Where else can we go with this line of questioning? Yeah, but, c'mon, really, Purito

– all those teams you rode for, your nationality, is that all you can say? Can't you say something more, y'know, inspirational to make us all feel better? We hacks in the press room would all be much happier with your impressive ride – wherein your team took responsibility for the race and you delivered a killer move in spite of the close attentions of your rivals – if it came with a statement that was a bit stronger on the anti-doping, pro-clean cycling line.

But then, is there a point to asking anything more? Have we a right to expect anything more? The fact is that 'Purito', for all the bad company he has kept, has never actually tested positive, and his performances have been fairly consistent. Without having access to a decade of his blood chemistry, a degree in haematology, his endocrinological profile and all his training data and tests, what more can be said? Even if Rodriguez went boldly on the record, saying he had never doped and never would, we still wouldn't really believe him. Such is the state of mistrust in 2012.

Drugs simply never went away – at all – during the 2012 season, all of which was played out against the gruesome backdrop of Lance Armstrong versus USADA and WADA [the World Anti-Doping Agency] with the UCI left looking inept at best, and deeply implicated at worst.

At Pau, on the rest day during the Tour, the most animated and excited many journalists got was when news of Frank Schleck's 'non-negative' for a

diuretic was announced. Never mind the Tour – there
was a doping story to sell even though, at 9pm on
a Tuesday night, there was no chance of any useful
facts emerging. Weeks later, we were still in the dark
over the drug in question, Xipamide. The frenzy of
tweets, web stories and speculation in Pau that summer night led to precisely no insights.

There was lots of sound and fury, all of it signifying nothing. Journalists scanning contact lists, daring each other to phone someone and ask a 'cheeky'
question along the lines of, 'So, when did you stop
beating your wife?' It was tabloid-esque: as in, the
only time the UK tabloid papers used to take any
interest in cycling was when there was a drug story.

This shift to a culture of suspicion and simmering hostility between media, teams and staff has not
been much aided by the other big changes in the sport
that have occurred in recent years: the team bus and
the press officer, both of which limit a journalist's
contact with riders. It's hard to build up a relationship of trust with rows of 18-ton customised Volvo
9700 buses with blacked-out windows and taped-off,
no-access exclusion zones. I hear Armstrong even
had bodyguards. Christ...

This loss of empathy and contact leads to
savage justice being meted out. There are no grey
areas these days, no more 'hormonal balancing and a
cortisone jag for tendinitis' any more.

The ethical rules on doping have been

re-written and if you waver on any issue, your entire project is suspect. Both
Jonathan Vaughters at Garmin and Dave Brailsford
at Sky have been explicit in their anti-doping positions, and both have had to compromise in some
areas, this being the real world we inhabit.

Vaughters is 'happy' to hire ex-dopers, and
'zero tolerance' Brailsford ended up hiring Dr
Geert Leinders, the doctor who was working with
Rabobank when the team's riders admitted to blood
doping. So, in spite of innumerable statements (and
deeds) that are expressly anti-doping, both men and
their teams still operate under suspicion or have their
motives endlessly questioned. This is a shock to me,
having come back to the sport from an era when
doping was never discussed to an era where not only
is it discussed but those who are outspoken in their
anti-doping sentiments are chastised for not doing
or saying enough. To come from an era when there
was zero transparency to an age where no amount of
transparency is sufficient to satisfy some observers
feels like we've fallen Through the Looking Glass.
More can always be said and done, but, Jesus Christ,
to pillory people who are making efforts in the right
direction is bewildering.

Bradley Wiggins, the winner of the 2012 Tour de
France, was asked incessant questions and subject to
many doubters during the Tour, cracked in one press
conference and cursed, swore and left the confer-

ence. There was outrage. How dare he? How dare
he tell his anonymous Twitter snipers to (paraphras-
ing) piss off? He was sick of it. Many in the press
were outraged. Few in the press room seemed able to
see it from Wiggins's point of view. At some point,
when your motives, training and history are quizzed
over and over, in every language, from every form
of media, every day, I reckon there comes a point
where any man would simply tell the world to 'do
one'. Where was the empathy or hint of understanding in his stressed out response? Many in the media
claimed they were hurt. Most fans reading about the
episode laughed and applauded. His 'rant' became a
T-shirt slogan of support.

Months later, after the Olympics, Wiggins spoke
of his Tour experience on Belgian television and still
seemed a bit stunned. 'I haven't come to terms with
the perception of people now that I've won the Tour
– that's what's changed,' he said. 'Winning the gold in
London was something I enjoyed more because the
Olympics is always just about the Olympics and the
people just loved it. There was no talk of doping or
any of the other rubbish that you have to deal with in
pro cycling. So it's just about the race and you win the
race and everyone is elated for you. It's just brilliant,
but the Tour is so stressful because all people want
to talk about is Twitter, doping and suspicions and all
this sort of stuff.

"So the Tour is a bit of drain and I think I showed

that when I crossed the line in the final time trial. I didn't enjoy the Tour this year. The Olympics were more enjoyable because it was purely about the sport and not all the other rubbish. Half the people who come to the Tour just come for a story and to talk about doping and everything else. And so the riders ultimately are the ones who have to answer those questions, and the Tour has become its own worst enemy in that regard. I'm pleased that I've won it now, and it is an incredible sporting achievement, but I ain't never ever going to miss all the other stuff that goes with leading the race – all the questions and responsibility that comes with it.'

* * *

The gigantism of the Tour de France, which has grown exponentially as a global phenomenon in the last 20 years is, it seems, taking a toll on its star riders. The need for people like press officers, therefore, is understandable in some ways, thanks to the sheer number of accredited journalists and media outlets wanting interviews with riders, but it sometimes seems that the press officer's role is to prevent the rider from talking to the media. The by-product of this, though, is a decrease in levels of empathy between riders and journalists, which breeds cynicism and distrust. Sometimes it's just unfathomable.

Picture the scene. You speak to a rider on the

morning of a grand tour and say, 'How about an interview at a time of your convenience?' And the rider says, 'Sure, no problem, come to the hotel tomorrow because today we've got a long transfer after the
stage today and we'd have more time the day after.'

Splendid.

Except that, in order to do the right thing and
not face excommunication by the team's management, you decide to email the press officer who is
not actually on the race, but five time zones away.
You email. You get no reply. You try to square things
up with the *directeur sportif.* That helps, but we need
the press officer to clinch the deal, for all our sakes.
But there's still no reply to the email to the press
officer (requesting an interview with a rider who says
he is happy to talk, remember).

Sod it.

Two days later, you turn up at the team hotel
and 'bump into' the *directeur sportif.* 'Have you had an
email back yet?' he asks.

'No, not yet. I don't know why.'

Pause.

'You know, the rider is sitting in reception. If you
were to go in and spot him and do what you need to
do, there's not a lot I can do about it, is there?'

'Err, no.'

The *directeur sportif*'s parting shot? 'Yeah, but I
don't know anything about this, okay?'

Walk into the hotel, spot the rider and arrange

a time after dinner. Do the interview. Next day, the *directeur sportif* shrugs. 'Sometimes there are things happening on this team that I really don't understand.'

That it should come to this – that two consenting adults can't agree to a conversation for a magazine feature and do it. We are now in a situation where a team wouldn't trust the rider to decide if he was too tired or stressed to speak to a journalist and a magazine that he either did or did not want to talk to.

So it is that journalists with limited access to riders and hacked off with anodyne press releases are emboldened to ask endless, relentless doping questions. Riders are under scrutiny like never before, social media is hijacking and bypassing legitimate journalism and press officers are acting as human shields to protect riders from all media other than tame TV. And to this ferment we need to add the plethora of internet content providers desperate to get a scoop or a scandal, quick to amplify rumour and cast aspersions in the hope of seeing a big spike on their unique-visitor numbers. This is where we are.

One recently retired British rider, now a *directeur sportif* at Garmin noted that: 'When I turned pro in 2000 and you saw an accredited British journalist on a race somewhere in Europe, you figured that he had some credibility – because he had the wherewithal to travel to the race and he had been given a press pass. Well, these days I can be interviewed by a guy with an iPhone perched on his shoulder doing something for a website that I've never heard of. There are so many of these people out there, running websites or blogs from their bedrooms in their parents' houses. And they come and ask about doping and I just think, "No thanks – I don't want me or my riders to get sucked into that." If you do talk about it all of a sudden you are that guy who is good for a doping quote and everyone comes to you. And then you are caught up in that media blender. I mean, really? You want that? Every day?'

* * *

Joaquim Rodriguez had a good year. After winning Flèche Wallonne, the Spanish rider then finished second overall at the Giro, won three stages at the Vuelta, led the race and finally finished third overall behind comeback-rider Alberto Contador and Alejandro Valverde. Rodriguez capped the year by winning Il Lombardia – as we must now call it – and topping the UCI ProTour individual rankings.

Rodriguez's press conference in Lecco following Il Lombardia was a far more sedate affair compared to the one after Flèche Wallonne. 'What have you changed to have such a stand-out season?' I asked. A new coach, a diet, training with a power meter?

'I've been consistent this year, but my performances haven't really changed in the last three years,' replied Rodriguez, causing this reporter to suffer from brain freeze and – fatefully – pause too long to ask a follow-up question.

Nobody else in the room was inclined to question Rodriguez's sense of 'consistency' and, in the mini scrum of iPhone flashes that followed, a Spanish 'journalist' emerged with her Lombardy press pass autographed on the back by Rodriguez.

'Historic!' she beamed. Tragic, I thought. In my view, that's nothing to do with journalism, so perhaps it's not so surprising that teams need press officers.

* * *

So, 14 years on, what's changed? Yes, the sport is cleaner (based on slower race speeds and a flattening of performances) and there's more information out there on cycling than at any point in history. Now I can watch the Critérium du Dauphiné live on my laptop, and don't have to buy a two-day-old copy of *L'Equipe* from a Glasgow city-centre newsagent to find out Robert Millar's results. And yet, for journalists, it's harder to get 'quality' time with riders than ever before, and we're forced to rely on press-release quotes and to fire booby-trapped, scoop-seeking questions in press conferences.

The other element in the culture of cycling that has changed is the sense in which doping has gone from being a taboo subject to the most important subject. And I find myself in the position of not really wanting to read about it any more – from being starved of information in 1992 to being utterly swamped by details about method and efficacy. We've come a long way. The practices and people we suspected were dubious? Yeah, guess what, they were doped cheats and some of the guys we thought were 'good' turned out to be 'bad', and lots of others operated in a morally ambiguous state somewhere in between. And of course some poor souls were riding clean but in all the bloody mess and steamroller rumour, we've forgotten about them.

The 2012 season was a hectic one, with its endless confessionals, journalists out for revenge, riders and managers hounded and harassed, and cycling spilling its guts over and over. But can we now move on and write a bit more about great performances again?

At the Vuelta one morning, I was idly chatting to Ben Swift of Team Sky about sprinting, or the weather, or tapas, and, although it was the day that Armstrong 'threw in the towel' in his fight with USADA, not for a second did I think about asking Swift what he thought. What was he going to say? What could he say that would add to the sum of knowledge? He looked about 15 years old and he never raced in the most polluted and corrupt decade of the sport. For riders of Swift's generation, it really is rapidly receding history. I might as well have asked him about his position on Laurent Fignon and the therapeutic use of cortisone, or about Jacques Anquetil's ethical stance on amphetamines and training.

We are none of us as naïve as we used to be, and it's great that we can ask the questions when they need to be asked but, please God, it's not the only story in town – not any more.

We've got access to data and information in a way that simply wasn't possible 14 years ago and, among the howls emanating from the bottomless pit of the web, there are also fantastic sources and people capable of providing insight and enlightenment. I am not – repeat not – trying to bury bad news or pretend everything is great in the garden, but the sheer volume of articles about doping (now that we are 'allowed' to talk about it) is in danger of drowning out the massive progress that's been made by some teams in changing the culture of the sport.

So, 14 years on, is pro cycling better or worse? Come on – I arrived back in cycling just in time to see the first-ever British winner of the Tour de France, and that's much, much better.

Talk about good timing...

Kenny Pryde was born in Glasgow in 1960. Scottish cycling correspondent for *Cycling Weekly* from 1987, he edited *Winning* magazine from 1991 to 1994 and was a staff writer on *Cycle Sport* and *Cycling Weekly* until 1998, after which he spent 14 years writing about mountain bikes and motorbikes before returning to his first love, part Lazarus, part Rip Van Winkle, in April 2012, having cunningly avoided Lance Armstrong's glory years.

12

Alasdair Fotheringham charts the career of Oscar Freire – the Spanish rider who retired at the end of the 2012 season.

Freire is an enigmatic figure who, despite winning the world champion's rainbow jersey and Milan-San Remo three times each, perhaps did not get the recognition his results deserved.

So, who is the real Oscar Freire?

THE EXILE

BY ALASDAIR FOTHERINGHAM

It was the wrong way for Oscar Freire to end his career, and yet in some ways it could not have been more appropriate: standing in a muddy field somewhere in Holland, cursing his Spanish team-mates at the end of his last World Championships for going back on their agreement to support him as sole leader on the final lap.

In one sense, Freire has always been isolated from his compatriots thanks to his success in races – the Classics, the Worlds – whose worth they have consistently failed to appreciate. And, at the 2012 World Championships in Valkenburg, for one last time that lack of recognition that had dogged him ever since he turned pro more than a decade before became bitterly clear.

In fact, it still remains. Not one homage has been held in Spain for Oscar Freire – three-time world champion, three-time winner of Milan-San Remo, Spain's first-ever winner of the Tour de France's green jersey, a winner of Ghent-Wevelgem and Paris-Tours – since he confirmed he was retiring from cycling, just minutes after the finish of his last race in Valkenburg.

But should we be so surprised? Ever since Federico Martin Bahamontes took a breakthrough victory at the 1959 Tour de France, Spain has been obsessed with stage racing. The Classics are treated with scant regard, and for years their results rarely garnered more than a paragraph or two in its sports dailies. Indifference overlaps with ignorance, too: I can recall sitting in the back seat of a car at the Tour de France once, whilst in the front Spain's two top cycling journalists had a prolonged argument about who had won Paris-Roubaix three months earlier. (They finally agreed it was either Johan Museeuw, forgetting he'd retired five years before, or the late Franco Ballerini – also long retired at the time.)

On an international level, though, in terms of results Freire had few equals in cycling. Indeed, he could have triumphed in Valkenburg if the Spanish team had stuck to the script. It would have been difficult, given the way Philippe Gilbert blasted clear on the final climb, but not impossible if Spain's Alejandro Valverde had not disobeyed team orders and instead stayed with Freire to lead him out rather than striking out on his own to win bronze.

A fourth world title for Freire would have been an historic moment for cycling and could have given a much-needed boost to the sport's flagging public profile in Spain.

Freire could have become the first man to win the World Championship road race four times, climbing ahead of Merckx, Binda and Van Steenbergen.

Had he won, he would have carried on for one final season, to honour the rainbow jersey. It could have been one final curtain call but instead, let down by his team-mates, Freire returned to his home in Switzerland, to his wife Laura and two children, and started planning his transition to the 'real world'.

The fact he calls Switzerland home these days makes him an exile and an outsider, but there are other facets of his character the Spanish seem incapable of appreciating.

Over the past decade, the number of their cycling stars stained by doping scandals has reached embarrassingly high levels. Freire stands out, yet again, as one of the handful of top Spanish racers to remain untarnished by the issue of banned drugs.

Freire has won at least one race in each of his 15 years as a professional and has a total of 72 victories to his name and yet he never quite broke through into the Spanish consciousness, certainly not in the way that the grand tour contenders have done.

While the rest of the world gasped at his ability to clinch the most audacious of victories – such as when he snatched Milan-San Remo from Erik Zabel's grasp when the German was already celebrating in 2004, or the time he bunny-hopped a traffic island to win a stage of the 2006 Tour of

Switzerland, or (a personal favourite this) scooting round the outside of a roundabout in the Trofeo Luis Puig while the peloton trundled round the other side and emerged to see Freire 200 yards up the road – in Spain, most of the time, they were left cold.

Sprinting doesn't capture the imagination in the same way that climbing does and even Freire's status as one of the best did little to change this.

A placid, easygoing individual most of the time, Freire masked his irritation at the lack of attention his achievements garnered. I can recall his anger getting the better of him only once, after becoming the first, and so far only, Spaniard to win Ghent-Wevelgem in 2008.

Outside Spain, though, he had a wide circle of admirers – among them, Mark Cavendish, who cited Freire as 'one of two riders in the peloton who would invariably be able to ambush me for a win each year'. As for the fans, as Freire puts it ironically, 'There's a far greater chance of someone stopping me for an autograph in Belgium or Holland than there ever will be in Spain.'

Only in his home town, Torrelavega, is there some kind of recognition, although even that seems a little grudging. They named their local velodrome after him – which is pretty much the least they could do.

Sports scientists raved about Freire, though, as soon as they started testing his physiological capacity.

'He's unique,' said the late Aldo Sassi, the long-standing trainer at Mapei, Freire's second pro team. 'He has the body of a climber, 1.71 metres tall and 65 kilos, but he's a sprinter and he can produce huge amounts of power in a short distance,' said Sassi.

'We analysed his performance in a sprint and, in 12 or 13 pedal strokes, he gained between seven and 10 metres on his rivals,' Sassi marvelled. 'It's something out of the ordinary.'

Physical talent was combined with a *savoir-faire* in stage racing that took the form of staying out of sight (and mind) until the crucial moment of a race. It made him a formidable rival, and he was very much respected in the peloton.

'You never even notice he's in the race,' said Paolo Bettini, himself a double world champion. 'And then you turn around in the last few kilometres and he's right at the front. Always.'

The one time even the Spanish sat up and noticed Freire was there, of course, was when he produced his first major win, in the 1999 World Championships at Verona. With just one minor victory to his name as a professional beforehand, Freire was the least-known factor in the leading break, and he gambled on nobody following him when he skittered away on the far side of the road with 700 metres to go.

Few in the race knew who he was and, to their cost, they hesitated. Freire calls it his 'most intelligent victory'. Not bad, to misquote Bradley Wiggins, for a working-class kid from one of the roughest areas of an ugly industrial town. And even better for a kid who contracted tuberculosis aged three – and whose doctors only decided at the last moment not to amputate one of his legs.

Freire was riding for Vitalicio Seguros, one of the smaller Spanish teams, when he won his first world title but the rainbow jersey attracted attention from some of the bigger squads in his home country.

However, it was Mapei, the Italian super squad that swept up all the talented Classics riders, who swooped for his signature. From that day, Freire never raced for a Spanish team again. Instead, he enjoyed a self-imposed exile in Italy, then with the Dutch Rabobank team and finally with the Russians at Katusha.

The Spanish Once team was interested before Freire won the world title, he says, but that victory pushed the asking price too high for a man who could have been perceived as a flash in the pan at the time.

But if failure to appreciate his stature and achievements dogged Freire's career, provided it did not affect his racing chances – as arguably it did in Valkenburg – he was wise enough not to care too much. Freire was never too big on cultivating the image of a cycling star; he's too practical and unpretentious for that.

Take his attitude towards his first World Championship title, for example. When I visited him, after the Worlds in 1999, the fabled rainbow jersey got no special treatment. The first glimpse I got of his new striped jersey was one hanging on a washing line among the rest of the family's washing.

The surroundings were a little down at heel. The family home in Torrelavega was a flat in a tower block, four floors up, where he still lived with his parents, a small tribe of brothers and his ageing grandmother. (If you look at pictures of Freire before he went up to collect his Worlds medal, he's listening to somebody on his mobile phone. It was his grandmother, singing him a regional folk song, as she always did each time he called after winning a race.)

A few months later, Freire turned up to his first training camp with Mapei, home to a host of more sophisticated and glamorous operators. Michele Bartoli, the Italian Classics ace, was aghast to learn that the Spaniard had driven there in something as singularly unshowy as a six-year-old Opel Corsa – Freire's one and only car.

More than a decade later, Freire still has it. Rather than spending his money on cars, a large chunk of Freire's first wages had been spent on a down-payment for a new home for his family.

'I wanted to get them a flat in a block with a lift in it, so my grandmother could get out and about,' he told me at the time.

But then Freire was always a one-off, a true individualist. It showed, particularly, in his refusal to follow trainers' advice, for example, believing he had developed enough sense over the years to do what was right for him, to the despair of his teams.

'I remember him turning up for a Rabobank training camp in very early January and telling us he'd been back on the bike and training hard for the new season – since the day after Christmas,' Rabobank's Adri Van Houwelingen says, indicating that Freire had little over a week of proper preparation under his belt before meeting up with his team. 'But that was Oscar.'

They could hardly criticise him, given his ability to get results. Prior to his first Worlds win in Verona, Freire used the roads around Torrelavega to design a circuit as similar as possible to the Italian course, and then trained on it day in, day out, come rain or shine.

'He had a reputation for being lazy,' Pedro Horrillo, his one long-standing domestique and team-mate for nine years, says. 'But I know Oscar, and when he got the bit between his teeth and had an objective in mind, he would train like an animal.

'When he used to quit the Vuelta a España and go home to train for the Worlds,' Horrillo continues, 'it wasn't because the Vuelta was too hard. It was because the racing wasn't tough enough.'

Freire was equally back-to-basics and independent-minded when it came to nutrition.

'When you do more [training], eat more; when

you do less, eat less,' was how he described his eating plan once, enough to put the entire dieting industry out of business.

And, unlike many other sprinters who are famous for being self-centred, fussy and given to the odd temper tantrum, one reason Freire was popular at Rabobank was that he would never complain about what turned up on the dinner table during races. Put simply, he never considered himself better than anyone else.

'He would conform with whatever was given to him. [Mario] Cipollini might have thrown a fit because he had the wrong food,' Horrillo recalls, 'but that wasn't the case with Oscar. Everything was okay, and it was the same with the mechanics, the soigneurs and with the management. I really don't think he ever made any enemies.'

Only one food appeared to break down Freire's resolve completely: yoghurts.

'Oscar was nuts about them,' Horrillo reveals. 'He would always carry a spoon in the glove compartment of his car so that if we happened to see one in a supermarket that he hadn't tried before, nothing could stop him from eating it.'

During his years at Rabobank, Freire never enjoyed the same level of support that other top Classics riders and sprinters would take for granted. At most, Horrillo would give him a lead-out, but that would be it. Yet if Freire had to fend for himself when it came to the elbows-out, rough-and-tumble world of bunch sprinting, he never had a reputation for foul play, unlike other lone sprint stars. Cavendish recalls once getting into a bit of argy-bargy with Freire, and was left feeling more amazed than worried about the outcome of their tussle, 'because Freire never, ever used to do stuff like that'.

'I've had my fair share of injuries,' Freire points out when discussing his career. His various problems – from nasal surgery to groin strains – have all added up to more than a season off the bike. 'But only once, just before I won the Vuelta a Andalusia [in 2007], when I had one physical problem after another, mainly back problems, did I ever think that I was going to have to quit the sport.'

'His health was the only thing he was fussy about, but that was because he'd been through so many doctors that he ended up only trusting one person,' Horrillo says – and that was Freire himself.

'At one Tour he completely destroyed half his saddle so that he could sit comfortably on it because he had an injured bone in his pelvis,' Horrillo recalls. 'The mechanics were horrified, but Oscar was determined that was the right thing to do.'

In the early spring of 2007, though, even Freire was close to cracking. 'I was feeling really depressed, and didn't know what to do, yet my form was good and the results kept coming. That's what encouraged me to continue.

'I never once fell off my bike in a sprint in 15 years as a pro, and I think that says something about the way I raced,' he says. 'It could be because I was lucky, but I also think it was because I respected others. You have to take risks, but I always knew which moments were the right ones and which ones were the wrong ones. There are too many crashes these days because riders are so nervous, so disrespectful towards each other. There was a certain degree of respect in the bunch when I started racing, but now that's gone. There are now so many guys that are doing well that even if they can't necessarily win, they can certainly help make you lose. To win you have to keep a cool head and, above all, race straight.'

There were other reasons for Freire's success.

'He was nicknamed The Cat, but he was more like a panther,' says Van Houwelingen. 'He'd be invisible in the peloton, waiting and waiting for his moment. And then, in one single moment – blam! – he'd stretch out his paw to take what he wanted.'

'People would forget he was there; they'd make the mistake of underestimating him,' recalls Italy's Dario Cioni, now retired, but who raced with Freire at Mapei. 'It was like he was asleep. And then suddenly, just at the right moment, he'd wake up to be on the right side of the break or the sprint.'

'It was like a sixth sense,' adds Horrillo. 'You'd ask him how he did it, but he wouldn't be able to explain how he had suddenly realised something was going to happen in the race. But he would. In the Tour, he could often tell you what would happen tomorrow, and nine times out of 10, he'd be right.'

Freire's intuition made him an unusual leader to work for, Horrillo says: 'I remember in the 2002 Tour when I was in charge of leading him out, he'd say, "We'll hook up with 40 kilometres to go," and then for the next 30 kilometres it'd be him looking after me! He'd be able to accelerate hard, even with 40 kilometres to go, and still have the strength left to sprint at the finish.

'We'd move up with about 10 kilometres to go, Oscar still guiding, and it was only with five kilometres to go that I'd take over, with him following me. But I wasn't really his lead-out man; I'd get him in position, and then what he did best from there was let other riders take the initiative – then get past them in the last 30 metres. That's what he did against Zabel at the 2004 Milan-San Remo. Oscar was like Robbie McEwen – he didn't need a lead-out train. What he missed most at Rabobank at the Tour were riders to support him earlier on – like me.'

To be able to pull off the 'trick' of out-sprinting rivals at the last moment – winning, as it were, with the last card – doesn't only require high levels of self-confidence; it also requires something Freire had in spades: tenacity.

'He was stubborn,' explains Cioni. 'If you tried to make him change his mind about something, he'd dig his feet in even harder. Oscar always knew what he wanted.'

'I was always learning, every time I went into a race,' Freire says. 'Too many riders these days repeatedly make the same mistake. But not me.'

Part of that natural tendency to educate himself was that Freire's family had no history in cycling. He was the first to show an interest. 'I didn't have idols as a young amateur because, to be perfectly honest, I knew nothing about the sport.'

Besides, in Spain, if you want to learn about the cobbled Classics, you must do your own research. They are barely covered.

On a training camp with the Vitalicio Seguros team, Horrillo remembers the sports director, Javier Minguez, saying: 'We need volunteers for Flanders and Paris-Roubaix,' which illustrates how popular those races were with the Spaniards.

'Nobody raised their hands except for me and Oscar. The rest of the team killed themselves laughing: they thought we were crazy to want to go and race there, because for them racing Flanders was a punishment. Oscar and I, in fact, were delighted.'

Even with his senior team-mates laughing at him, Freire was never afraid of speaking his mind – he once called the Tour de France 'a boring race'.

But when dealing with matters outside racing, his willingness to put his head above the parapet is even more noticeable.

As world champion, he was by far the most high-profile of the handful of riders in the entire peloton – 11 or 12 out of 180 – who supported a general strike in Spain in 2002, refusing to race the bulk of that day's stage in the Volta a Catalunya. Then, in 2007 as race leader of the Tour of Spain, he attacked the UCI for being 'a business that failed to look after the riders' interests, instead just exploiting them'.

He also refused to automatically back compatriot Alberto Contador in the Tour winner's clenbuterol case – not the easiest of attitudes to take in Spain, where Contador is a national hero – instead adopting his own, very individual point of view on it.

'He could be guilty, he could be innocent,' Freire said in early 2012. 'I'm not putting my hand in the fire for anybody.

'The [two-year] suspension [for Contador] isn't very fair,' he continued, 'but the rules are what they are in cycling; nobody's done anything to change them and if you're a cyclist that's what you have to obey. It doesn't matter if we're right or not.'

He states, matter-of-factly, to me that his 15 years of racing without the remotest hint of a doping problem 'is something that is not valued'.

'Well, probably some fans do value it,' he adds, 'but at the end of the day it's the results that count. If something [a doping scandal] happens, then you're a delinquent and a cheat, but up until that date, everybody's viewed equally. Nobody's going to value it [my clean record] ever, but I feel proud that I could win a lot of races and do very well despite my misfortune of having lived through this particular era of cycling.'

Not that he had any real faith in the 'system' governing cycling, pointing out that 'anti-doping tests aren't carried out in a secure way. The UCI does what it wants'. He was also one of the few riders to protest – for common-sense reasons, rather than ethical ones – against the imposition of the where-abouts system.

'But that was the last time I put up a fight,' he told Spanish newspaper *AS* this spring. 'I told the team it was unacceptable and they told me I had to sign it to be paid. I realised then that everybody does what they want and they all seemed to find it normal.'

Freire's opposition to ADAMS [Anti-Doping Administration and Management System], which requires athletes to make themselves available for an out-of-competition test for one hour of every day, was relentlessly logical.

'There can be situations where it gets complicated, like when they give you a "strike" because you're in an area without phone coverage... I haven't done anything to be treated like a suspect.'

For those that have committed a doping offence, though, Freire believes the UCI should be more ruth-less, calling for lifetime bans for EPO use, 'because it isn't fair we all end up with the same image'.

At the same time, he was willing to concede that a large part of the responsibility for cycling's poor reputation was a result of the sport's own errors. 'People think badly of the cycling profession,' he once said, 'and they are right to do so.'

Freire's attitude to the ADAMS system is very much the same as the one he has towards life in general: one of extreme practicality.

'His father's wages – three times less than what he could make, or twice, or whatever – were the yardstick he'd use whenever he had a financial question to resolve,' Horrillo says. 'I think it was a good system. He'd be racing in some awful town in Holland, it'd be tipping down with rain and if he got a bit gloomy he'd start comparing what his dad earned in Torrelavega with what he was earning for one hour's racing.'

It is perhaps surprising that somebody so astute on the bike and canny in his financial affairs could be as forgetful as Freire. Yet his ability to mislay everything was legendary.

'It was even worse in reality,' laughs Horrillo. 'It got to the point where we'd play tricks on him, telling him he'd lost things when he hadn't.'

Things that went missing while in Oscar's possession ranged from the merely trivial, like race numbers, cycling shoes, his passport and mobile phones, to losing himself and his bike for five hours in Lisbon during the Worlds build-up (he had to ask a taxi driver to take him back to the team hotel, the only problem being that he had forgotten the name, remembering only it was 'white and had a swimming pool'). Losing his passport three times en route to Marrakech for a family holiday was one of the most famous episodes of the 'forgetful Freire' stories. Another was driving 200 kilometres to pick up his mislaid racing licence from a friend's house, getting his attention diverted by the number of different yoghurts the friend had in his fridge (which he promptly devoured) and then driving all the way home again. Without the licence.

There is even a rumour Laura, now his wife, was on the point of ditching him after three months of going out together because he could never remember her name, but that could be an exaggeration.

Minguez once joked: 'Oscar Freire doesn't get lost at the World Championships because it's the only race in the world with barriers around the whole circuit.'

Even Minguez was wrong. Freire in fact did get lost while training with his team on the circuit in Verona prior to taking the title a few days later.

Yet Freire's natural talent was something not even he could mislay. And this, it should be emphasised, was as a Classics rider with a huge capacity for sprinting, rather than a pure sprinter who happened to have a talent for the Classics.

'My first big win as an amateur was the Memorial

Valenciaga, Spain's top one-day race, and that's really hilly,' he points out. 'I beat some top climbers that day – like Francisco Mancebo, Carlos Sastre and [the 2003 world champion] Igor Astarloa.'

A silver medal in the under-23 road race at the 1997 Worlds was the key to his first professional contract with Vitalicio Seguros.

'I had a very good first year as a pro, but when they wanted me to sign another contract at the end of that first year, I refused,' says Freire.

It was a standard tactic at the time: managers would force neo-pros, contracted by law for two seasons, to extend their deal beyond their 'rookie' first year to a third or fourth year, but often for the same money or only a small rise.

Freire's first pro season had included bronze at the Spanish national championships behind two team-mates, and 17th at the World Championships on an exceptionally difficult course in Holland.

'Although I had a second year with a lot of injuries, I finished second in my first race back [the GP Cuenca] and then went to the Worlds where the Spanish national team manager [Paco Antequera] had a lot of faith in me.'

Yet it all could have turned out so badly.

'Antequera saw what Oscar could do in the Worlds the previous year and told him that if he recovered in time, he'd be part of the squad,' recalls Horrillo. 'But when it turned out that Oscar was one of the

Vitalicio riders taking part, Minguez called up Antequera and told him he didn't want Oscar to go.'

Minguez was convinced Freire had already signed with another team for the 2000 season and was furious with him for 'faking' injuries. But they were anything but fake.

'I remember we did Paris-Brussels two or three weeks before the Worlds and Oscar did a good race. But then, on the way back on the plane, he was asking for ice from the air hostess because his back was hurting him so much,' Horrillo recalls, before using a motoring metaphor to explain Freire's propensity for injuries. 'I think maybe one of his problems was that he had too big an engine for his chassis. But on the plane he looked at me and said, "I'm going to do a good Worlds."'

'Once we got to the Worlds, I was looking at him and I realised he was going really well,' continues Horrillo. 'But that final attack – that was a stroke of genius. The funny thing is, you ask him, "How did you do it?" and he still doesn't know. It just came out of him.'

'If I hadn't won the Worlds that year [1999], I'd have won it another year,' is how Freire sees it. 'Before the race that year, I didn't think I would win but I had the mentality of a winner. And I'd learn quickly. When I was a junior they took me to a race and we were put in the same competition as the under-23s, and for the first time in my life I raced in crosswinds and echelons. That day I was in the back group. But I learned how they'd done it, how the breaks had gone, and so on. The next time there was an echelon in a race I was in, I was a pro, and I was at the front. I learned from my mistakes. Others could be strong as hell but they wouldn't learn.

'Some riders would suffer simply to get through a race, even to finish it,' he continues. 'That wasn't my case – winning was, logically enough, the hard part. But you can see that I've always been a very consistent rider – never riding much above my usual level but never much below it.'

In 2012, even though he only won three races – two stages in Andalusia and one at the Tour Down Under – Freire had a long string of top-10 results. Second in the E3 Harelbeke, second in Flèche Brabançonne (a race he won four times – an all-time record), fourth at Ghent-Wevelgem and Amstel Gold (which he was on the point of winning with a spectacular late, lone break), seventh in Milan-San Remo and – most painfully of all – 10th in the most emblematic of all 'his' races, the Worlds.

'The move to Katusha for the 2012 season did him a power of good and, combined with those results, I thought it might make him change his mind about retiring,' said Horrillo. 'But crashing in the Tour didn't help.' After that, Horrillo thought his friend was likely to call it a day.

Then, at the World Championships when the one

chance of delaying his departure went up in smoke, Freire was gone.

Freire's success at the World Championships – three titles in six years – almost undermined him. Remember, until Abraham Olano in 1995 Spain had never won the men's road race title at the Worlds.

Olano's victory owed everything to a rigid team policy with the entire squad – even Miguel Indurain – working for him.

In 2001 and, most spectacularly, in 2004, Freire was the undisputed head of the team, with lead-out efforts from Luis Perez and Valverde in Verona giving him the launchpad he needed for his third World Championships victory.

'Oscar's 2004 title was a real team victory,' says Horrillo, 'right down to the celebration afterwards. I was rooming with Oscar and, after I'd worked in the first part of the race and abandoned, I went up to the room and pretended to be asleep when he got in after winning, in the mood to celebrate. He didn't know that the entire team was in the bathroom with 10 bottles of champagne, waiting to surprise him.'

However, since then, as Freire sees it, 'the Worlds has got more and more popular, and more and more riders want to win it. That ends up with your rivals, as it were, being on your own team, just as happened in the Italian squad for many years.'

In 2012, on a course reminiscent of the Amstel Gold Race, Freire discovered to his cost the hidden division in the team when Valverde jumped away.

'In Spain we've got lots of riders who can win, because they come out of the Vuelta with good form,' he says. 'We did well right up until the last lap, but then what made me a bit angry was that we didn't race the way we had agreed. But those are things that you can't do anything about.'

He is philosophical about his lack of celebrity status or hullabaloo surrounding his retirement.

'The only homage I'm going to get is the one my wife is organising, bringing together my friends and the people who have been with me during my career. The kind of cyclist I am hasn't had much of an appeal,' he admits. 'It doesn't bother me too much. I don't expect anything from anyone.'

Yet if Freire disappears off the map in Spain, at least his results will remain. He came from fertile ground and conquered land hitherto uncharted by his compatriots. As he puts it, 'Everybody remembers those three World Championships, but I think I've done a lot more than that.'

It would be hard to disagree.

Alasdair Fotheringham is Spanish correspondent for *The Independent* and *The Independent on Sunday*, and covers cycling for both papers as well as *www.cyclingnews.com*, *Reuters*, *procycling* and the *Daily Express*. He has covered 21 Tours de France and the Beijing and London Olympics. His first book, a biography of climbing great and Tour de France 1959 winner Federico Martin Bahamontes, was published in 2012.

13

There have been precious few true characters in professional cycling, and fewer still capable of matching Mario Cipollini.

Samuel Abt recalls the Italian sprinter's flamboyancy and delves deeper into the ultimately aborted attempt by 'The Lion King' to make another comeback in 2012.

IL MAGNIFICO'S TWILIGHT

BY SAMUEL ABT

In his recent divorce, the flamboyant Italian Mario Cipollini lost his Tuscan villa and, presumably, the two cheetahs that he said he kept as pets. He still has his fast cars, a different pair of shoes for every day of the year, plus his many designer suits – so many, he has said, that he had not worn some even once.

He also still has the business that makes bicycle frames with his name on them. And certainly he has all those jerseys he won: the yellow jerseys from the Tour de France (where he took 12 stage victories, including an astonishing four consecutive stages in 1997), the pink one from the Giro d'Italia (where he won a record 42 stages), the rainbow jersey for winning the road race World Championships in 2002, as well as the trophy he received for winning Milan-San Remo in the same year.

All those memories and nicknames – Super Mario, The Lion King, *Il Magnifico*. Even, blush, The Italian Stallion. And the rest: that yellow bicycle he rode for two days in the 1997 Tour to match his jersey, and the green one he used when he hoped to snag the points jersey in 1998. All those jerseys, uniforms – the time trial skinsuit with his bones outlined, the one with a stylised lion motif – and costumes, including the toga he wore at the Tour de France to celebrate, so he insisted, Julius Caesar's birthday. What a blazing way to ward off a mid-life crisis for somebody who turned 45 in March 2012.

Not that he has been totally out of the swim. He continues to be sought out for comment by Italian journalists and, two years ago, after a long trial, he was found not guilty of evading income taxes.

Even better, in 2007 he was cleared of charges of running a brothel when he explained that the scores of women in the building were all former girl-friends.

'For my 40th birthday, I rented out a chateau and held a big bash there,' he said. 'And, to make it special, I invited some of my ex-girlfriends to be present for the weekend. It's obvious that one of the many past conquests I didn't invite called the police and spread these rumours. Ah, it's incredible what jealousy can do.'

So his recent life has not been without excitement. What was up, then, when Cipollini (meaning 'little onion' in Italian, as foodies well know) announced just before his latest birthday, and three years after his third retirement, that he hoped to return to the sport at the highest level? Not quite the highest level, actually: he no longer yearned to be the top sprinter, but a mere lead-out man for the Farnese Vini-Selle Italia team and its young hope Andrea Guardini.

'I want to return to racing to come to the Giro and lead out the sprints for Guardini,' he told the Italian newspaper *La Gazzetta dello Sport*. 'I feel good, and it's a good sign that I feel an extreme desire to work hard.

'I weigh 90 kilos – eight more than when I was in top condition – but it's not excess fat, just muscle, especially in my arms and trunk. My legs are perfect. I have some little pains in my knee and back, but my motor is good and capable of standing up to this gamble.

'Guardini has talent and races on my bikes,' he continued. 'It would really be a beautiful challenge to be one of his domestiques at the Giro and, if I pulled the sprint for him, how many would he win?'

He explained that he would also advance science, helping 'to understand what changes there are in a high-level athlete with the passing of years. I'm convinced that even someone of 45 years of age isn't to be dismissed as an athlete'.

Nevertheless, and alas, his wishes were quickly dismissed.

First to scoff was Luca Scinto, the *directeur sportif* of the Farnese Vini team, which Cipollini said he hoped to join.

'For me, it's a bolt from the blue. I really didn't know anything about it and I don't like it,' Scinto told

Tuttobiciweb. 'I respect Cipollini as a champion and a man, and I always will, but this really seems like a joke to me. What can I say? As long as I'm in charge of this team, we won't talk about it.'

Scinto added that he felt that the whole exercise was meant to generate publicity for Cipo's frames.

'If this is all a nice marketing ploy for his company, then he's succeeded in part, but cycling isn't only special effects and marketing,' Scinto said. 'What can I tell you? The team is full and there is no place for Mario. The boys don't need him – far less Guardini, who is a very promising young rider, but who needs to grow with calm and without distractions in his first Giro.'

Another obstacle was the regulation that any retired rider who wishes to return must notify the International Cycling Union six months in advance and spend at least four months on the anti-doping register. But that rule was waived in 2009 to allow Lance Armstrong to ride the Tour Down Under in his comeback from retirement.

Cipollini rejected suggestions that any return to cycling was motivated by financial gain.

Citing a close friend, the Formula One driver Michael Schumacher, Cipollini said: 'Schumacher has money, right? And a family? So who made him come back and risk his neck? Armstrong has come back into the fray in triathlons. There are conscious and unconscious factors. Above all, an athlete lives on emotions that are hard to leave behind.'

In a snit when his team was not invited to the Tour de France, Cipollini first retired in 2002 and unretired after a few months. In 2005, he retired again, but three years later came back to ride for US squad Rock Racing at the Tour of California before quitting again.

As for Cipollini's latest comeback attempt, Scinto appeared to voice the general feeling.

'Mario was a real great, but he's had his time,' he said. 'And it's right that he acknowledges that calmly himself. He is a very intelligent and sensitive person. If he reflects a bit, he too will understand that today was only a provocation, and I consider it as such.'

What, Mario Cipollini trying to provoke some excitement?

When the dust settled, Cipo's role was limited to a pre-Giro visit with the MCipollini-Giambenini-Gauss squad – a women's team – at Lake Garda for a day of training and tactical discussion. Cipollini's company supplies frames to the team.

'This sport needs more attention and much more professionalism,' said the team manager, Alessia Piccolo. 'To that end, I hope to have given my girls a nice present by putting a great champion like Mario Cipollini at their disposal. He passed on a lot to the athletes both in terms of training methods and the life of an athlete in general.'

In the Giro itself, Guardini won the 18th

stage, the final chance for sprinters, by beating the esteemed Mark Cavendish. Until then, Guardini had not figured in a sprint.

'I'm still very young and I've got to develop a lot as a rider,' Guardini explained. 'During the first week I didn't believe in myself enough. I'd been struggling in the sprints and things hadn't been going my way. The difference between winning and losing a sprint all comes down to experience.'

Who better to have supplied a dose of that experience than Cipollini? After the stage, he had no comment, which said a lot.

Samuel Abt is the first American to be awarded the Tour de France medal for service to the race. He began writing about bicycle racing in 1977 for the *International Herald Tribune* and the *New York Times* and continued there for more than 30 years. In 2012 he entered the hyperspace world with a Tour blog for *bicycling.com*. Abt has written 10 books about bicycle racing, including the pioneering *Breakaway* in 1985. Now retired as a newspaperman, he lives in France.

14

Jeremy Whittle followed Sky at the Tour of Romandy and found the pressure was getting to Bradley Wiggins weeks before he stepped into the pressure cooker of the Tour de France.

Like everyone else who wins in these days, Wiggins found every performance under scrutiny.

And it seemed the cynicism infecting the sport can be traced to one man.

Will the inability to trust be Lance Armstrong's lasting legacy?

BIN BAG OF MY DREAMS

BY JEREMY WHITTLE

I can't remember exactly where it was. Brixton, maybe – a flat somewhere down towards Herne Hill.

The end of the 1990s, or perhaps post millennium. Maybe winter 2000. There's wine on the table, rain falling outside the window, Travis's *Driftwood* playing in the background.

We're sitting around after dinner, a big group, and the girl next to me, pretty, smiley, happy, chatty, says, 'So, what did you say you do?'

I say, 'I'm a journalist, covering, erm, sport mainly.' Pause. 'Things like the Tour de France – you know it?'

She almost levitates with excitement.

'Oh God – the Tour? I love it, I love Lance Armstrong! He's amazing! Have you read his book?'

This is rare – somebody who likes cycling, and a woman, too. Even so, my heart sinks.

'Yes, well, I've only skimmed it really.'

'God, he's incredible. To win the Tour after all he's been through! My mum's just had treatment and she's reading his book... She loves it...' She smiles at me.

'You haven't... You haven't met him, have you?'

Oh Christ, here we go.

'A bit – well, a few times. Interviews and things.'

'Oh wow – no way, really? What's he like?'

Charismatic, arrogant, aggressive, rude – and sometimes a little scary.

'Oh, well, er, he's great,' I say. 'Funny, you know – pretty funny, pretty sharp, lots of dry wit. Yeah, he's amazing.'

For a while, every time I got asked, about the Tour, about The Legend of Lance, I lied.

I still told them I was a journalist, that I went to France a fair bit. For travel, though – to write about travel, not sport, not the Tour de France, not Lance Armstrong – travel, that's my game.

* * *

July 1995. Lance Armstrong's third Tour appearance, my second year on the race.

Ahead of us, 'The Cowboy' is stuck to the road. Halfway up the Cormet de Roselend, he is fighting the bike, fighting the gradient, his big rear end, all power but no *souplesse*, churns and churns, but it's no good. He can't hold the wheel. The break moves clear of him and he slumps back into the saddle, shoulders sagging.

The rest of the race convoy overtakes, leaves him, following the leaders, far up ahead, skipping around the hairpins that wind towards the Roselend's wild and beautiful summit.

Pretty soon, it's just us and Lance, plodding along.

It must have looked pretty odd to the fans lining the climb, this brawny American rocking in the saddle, followed by a right-hand drive Rover with British plates. And after a while even we lose interest, accelerating past, glancing across at him, his eyes glazed, the sweat dripping down his nose.

He can't climb, I think – not like he needs to. The Tour's always going to be too much for him.

Stage wins, that's the way to go for Lance Armstrong. Stage wins.

* * *

January 2012.

On a bar stool in the lounge of a deserted beach hotel in Mallorca, Dave Brailsford stares pensively out at the windswept Mediterranean. He turns the dregs of his espresso in a cup, and finally knocks it back.

The stars are aligned for Brailsford. Sky are poised to take control of the European scene. They have a leader, once reluctant and lacking in commitment, finally ready to realise his full potential. But if

he does, the same old suspicions, the same issues of
context, will cloud his achievements.

Out in the hills lining the north coast of the
island, a convoy of Sky team cars is following a
pencil-thin Bradley Wiggins and his team-mates
through a long and punishing climb, spinning their
way up past Lluc monastery and beyond, before
swooping down, through the switchbacks and hairpin bends, to Sa Calobra and the sea.

As Tour de France hopeful Wiggins and Sky's
new signing, world champion Mark Cavendish,
perfect their form, Brailsford, the architect of both
Team Sky and Team GB, sits quietly in the empty
lounge pondering the coming season, the 2012 Tour
de France and the London Olympics.

'That's the question isn't it?' he says after a long
pause.

'That's what we said we'd do. We said we'd win
the Tour with a British rider, that we'd win it clean.'

But has it really changed, Dave, I ask? Has it
really changed enough for that to happen?

'Yeah, it has,' he insists. 'I'm sure of it.'

Later, back from his five-hour ride in the
Mallorcan mountains, showered and recovered,
Wiggins is loafing around the team hotel with Sky's
coach, Shane Sutton. The Australian, once winner of
the Milk Race, has been out on the bike himself and
comes Lycra-clad, straight from the saddle, to join
Wiggins at the pool table.

Afterwards Wiggins sits down, mug of builder's tea in his hand, for a chat.

'These days, I think less and less about it,' he says of the doping culture that shadowed his earlier career. 'In 2006, 2007, it was a constant frustration. I always felt I was a little bit away from achieving something – I had a right chip on my shoulder back then.

'I was in a French team – all they used to talk about was who was on drugs. It was self-consuming, constant: "*Imagine what you could have done today if they hadn't been there.*"'

The next morning, under chilly winter skies, Wiggins and Cavendish are out on the road again, on another sortie into the hills, accompanied by a wide-eyed and starstruck band of VIP guests.

In the Team Sky people carrier following the knot of riders, the effervescent Sutton is, as ever, holding forth.

'You know what Cadel Evans gives his team-mates every time he wins a race?' he says of Australia's first-ever Tour de France winner. There's a long pause.

'A fucking Toblerone…' Everybody cracks up.

As Wiggins and Cavendish lead the breathless VIPs through the rolling landscape, Sutton debates the wisdom of the federal investigation into Lance Armstrong.

'What's the point?' he says tetchily. 'It's ancient

history. Leave the guy alone. It's just doing more damage to the sport. It's not going to fix anything.'

* * *

A few weeks later, after taking a red-eye to Basle, photographer Pete Goding and I get into another hire car and head off to follow Team Sky. This is race reporting, not investigative journalism, although increasingly the lines are blurred.

Recently, after spending some time studying form, I've been on a hot streak of near-misses. After staking £100 on Louis Oosthuizen to win the Augusta Masters – at 90/1, I might add – only to see Bubba Watson reach over and take the money out of my hand, I make a decision. I am never going to bet again.

Now, as I get out of the car outside another gymnasium, perched on a European mountainside, with Bradley Wiggins yet again in a yellow jersey, I've changed my mind.

I start to wish I'd put that 100 quid on him, Mr Grumpy, to win the Tour, back in January, when I'd first thought of it. At the moment, as the Tour of Romandy nears the finish of stage two, with Alberto Contador banned and the Schleck brothers AWOL, he's looking, well, a shoo-in.

We arrive so early at the finish that the race hasn't even left Montbéliard, where the stage starts. The deserted press room at the top of the Chemin de Piscine is ringed by forested hills, and huge tumbling verdant pasture. Below us is Moutier, an anonymous Swiss town in the Vaud.

The previous evening, after pulling off a surprise sprint win in La Chaux-de-Fonds, Wiggins had attended a shambolic press conference. You'd think, given that he was sitting in yet another yellow jersey at the head of the classification of yet another prestigious stage race, that he'd have been in relaxed mood.

Team Sky's website covered his success, and was full of cheery bonhomie from the Londoner. The reality, it emerged, as I worked my way around the room in a flurry of handshakes and '*ça vas*' was perceived as very different.

Wiggins, they said, had lost it with the avuncular Jean-Jacques Rosselet, the veteran *chef de presse* of the Swiss race.

'Cameron should use you as a spin doctor,' he'd said to Rosselet. 'You don't understand a word I'm saying, do you?'

He'd even, I was told, forgotten his own team-mates' names.

'Kanstantsin *quelque chose*,' he'd said dryly, as he described Sky's work ethic towards the end of the stage. 'Kanstantsin *something* – yeah, he brought me back.'

But it was his dismissive attitude that irritated

them most. 'Are we done yet? Maybe think about
some real questions for tomorrow, eh?'

If there's one thing the meticulously-mannered
Swiss don't like, it's rudeness.

Faced with hours to kill before the race arrives,
we go for a walk. 'Cav won't like this,' I think to myself, as the final kilometre swings up a sharp bend,
200 metres from the finish line.

As we wander around, Pete walks into the ice
rink alongside the finish line and studies a gloomy
collection of trestle tables set out in the middle of
the arena. 'I wish I'd played ice hockey, you know,'
he says wistfully.

By mid-afternoon in Moutier, the pavements, deserted at midday, are now crammed as spectators line
the road. A heavily pregnant teenager with Sharon
Osbourne hair and a too-short skirt, chain-smokes as
the peloton sweeps through, Wiggins's hapless team-
mate, Kanstantsin *quelque chose,* leading the bunch.

Once the race convoy has headed out into the
hills for the circuit before the final sharp haul to
the finish, the crowd disperses. I stumble upon the
Sky bus, but, as I head back to the press room, a
team helper emerges carrying a crammed black bin
liner. He ignores a nearby hopper and begins walking
down the road.

I follow him at a distance, folkloric tales of French
TV crews rummaging through rubbish, uncovering
syringes and blood bags, flooding back to me. He

carries the bag to a street corner, opposite a super-market, with a busy pavement café in the entrance, and pushes it into a bin. Just an ordinary street bin – the kind you might toss chewing gum, a fag packet, or an empty coffee cup, into.

Before the ethical makeover, searching team rubbish was de rigueur, particularly among the French media, when it came to Lance Armstrong's US Postal Service team. In fact, it became almost a sport in itself. That's how Actovegin, or '*Acto-wassisname*' as Lance once called it, came to light.

I hang back, then walk over. I look at the families sitting opposite, the buggies lined up, the babies on laps. Should I haul the bag out of the bin and begin ripping through it, in the hope of finding something that justifies my lingering damned cynicism? No, I decide, because that way lies madness.

I turn and walk back to the finish. A couple of hundred metres from the line, I run into Nick Howes, Sky's press officer, charged with recce'ing the finish by Sean Yates, who, like most of us, is no doubt won-dering if the final hill is too much for Cav.

'What do you think the percentage is?' he says.

'Not one for Cav, is it?' I say. 'Nine per cent on that bend, maybe.'

Instead, I'm thinking that maybe Cadel Evans, if he can find his legs again, can do something on this nasty little hill. Not that I'd put any money on it, of course.

Nick says that the previous day's press conference was a mess.

'Some French radio guy was heckling a bit and then they just ran out of questions. I think Bradley might be pleased to see a British journo, to be honest...'

Out on the second-category climb of La Caquerelle, with its nasty 12 per cent stretches, the breakaway is collapsing under pressure from Sky, and two big names – Evans and Cavendish – are struggling.

The bunch strings out, descending at 80 kilometres per hour through the forest in dappled spring sunlight, a glimpse of pro racing at its most beautiful. Wiggins is constantly shepherded by his Sky guard. A group, led by Peter Stetina of Garmin, eases ahead with a few kilometres to race. It won't last long.

They swing up towards the ice rink and Jonathan Hivert of France elbows his way through the chaos, punches the pedals as he squirrels up the hill and screams in delight as he crosses the line first. Wiggins, hidden in the bunch, is 40-odd places behind him. Cavendish comes in over eight-and-a-half minutes later.

Soigneurs, journalists and fans – one asking each breathless rider for their water bottle as a souvenir – cluster around the riders as Wiggins eases through the throng to be met by Nick Howes and guided to a home trainer behind the hastily thrown-up marquee that passes for a changing room.

This is something I have never seen at a stage race. Even Armstrong didn't do this – get back on a stationary home trainer within seconds of crossing the finish line. It is meticulous, and hints at Wiggins's track roots.

But maybe this is who Bradley really is – another elite rider with too many demons, finding at last what he really needs as the race ends, to feel the rage in his guts dissipate, to feel the waves breaking.

After five minutes' warm-down, in an alleyway behind the podium, he reappears, led by Howes.

'Brad's not doing a press conference tonight,' Nick says, a little unsurprisingly (and unnecessarily).

Which, in my book, is, like, a real shame, given the pleasingly exciting questions my Swiss colleagues had diligently prepared for him since being ticked off the day before!

Instead, I sit in on another short session of tense questions, posed in broken English by Swiss radio, answered tetchily and impatiently by Wiggins. From where I'm standing, it doesn't look as if the warm-down is working. The more dismissive he is, the more anxious the questioner becomes.

Here's an unedited transcript:

Swiss radio chap: 'After the stage, you make a kind of "after-cycling"?'
Bradley Wiggins: 'Yeah, bizarre isn't it? What can I say? It's not complicated, you know. It's a warm-down.

You finish like that, you're angry – you wanna punch people in the face, and it's just good to do 10 minutes warming down, easy, for tomorrow. I need to get back to the hotel, eat, rest, massage, sleep. The warm-down is just 10 minutes for myself straight afterwards because everybody's pulling me, left, right, can you do this? Can you do that?'

Swiss radio chap: 'Your team is leading from the first day...'

Wiggins: 'You're very perceptive. I have the yellow jersey, that's correct...'

Swiss radio chap: 'You come here to win in Romandy?'

Wiggins: 'I don't race much any more, and when I do, I race to win.'

He stands up and walks, uninterrupted by fans or journalists, through the throng and heads for a waiting team car. Later there are more stories doing the rounds of an angry Wiggins pushing away the anti-doping chaperone, so intent was he on his warm-down.

'He's nervous, isn't he?' says one Swiss journo. 'That's why he's so angry.'

But what does he mean – why would Wiggins be nervous?

We hang around in the press room, working until about eight, before packing up.

As we drop back down, past the winding ramps

to the finish, and into Moutier, I give in to the devil – the Kimmage, if you will – on my shoulder and ask Pete to make a left and swing past the supermarket and café. Both are closed now. The families and buggies, the buses and the team cars, have long gone and the back streets of Moutier are deserted.

We pull over and, for a moment, sit, engine running, in silence. Yes, this is a kind of madness, I think, a kind of creeping delusion, this damned suspicion. This is the legacy of Lance.

We reverse around the corner into the supermarket car park. The bin is empty. Of course it is. This is Switzerland. Let's keep it tidy. What was I thinking?

'Ready?' says Pete, struggling to stifle laughter.

'Fuck off and drive,' I tell him.

* * *

The next afternoon, after Luis Leon Sanchez has taken a typical *puncheur*'s win in an uphill sprint in Charmey, Wiggins again seems determined to avoid the media, sitting glumly in the changing-room-marquee thing behind the podium and then making the quickest possible exit after stepping up to pull on yet another yellow jersey.

Nick Howes looks on, a pained expression on his face.

'Nick – is he doing a press conference?' I ask.

'Nah,' Nick says.

'Any radio?' I suggest, hopefully.

'Nope...'

I can't help laughing.

After stepping down from the podium, Wiggins snaps impatiently at Howes, asking where the team's hotel is.

As it happens, Sky are tonight sleeping only 100 metres from the finish line, in the Hotel Callier, which, with its high terraces, has a damn-fine view of famed local beauty spot, the Maleson mountain. As the riders troop through reception, Euro-trash music booms from a nearby beer tent.

The good news for Wiggins is that the hotel is also the site of the *salle de presse*. Even so, still determined to avoid the hordes of Wiggins maniacs dogging his every move, he slips out of the race leader's jersey and reverts to the British champion's jersey.

Half an hour later, I'm making a coffee in the Nespresso machine in the hotel foyer when Cav comes in, pulling his wheely bag, remonstrating, calmly but pleadingly, with a race *commissaire*.

'It's not like I'm fat or something, or not been training,' I hear Cavendish say, although it's not clear if it's an apology or a justification.

There's a problem for Wiggins, though. The race organisation have told him he has to come to the press room. As his room in the Hotel Callier is all of two floors up, Sky have little chance to refuse.

Ten minutes later, still in kit, with a sullen look on

his face that reminds me of a chastened seven year old, he sits down. I can see in his eyes immediately that he hates being here.

I ask the first question, then the second. I wait for anybody else to pipe up. There is a heavy silence. Are they boycotting him after what happened in Moutier, I wonder?

Eventually, there is one question in French, and one more from me, which gives him a chance to eulogise Cavendish's efforts, on his behalf, during the stage.

'He was making a lot of people hurt,' Bradley says.

Yeah, mate, maybe, but it wasn't as painful as this...

Then it's over and he stands up, although there's still time for a parting shot.

'Your complaint worked,' he shouts across the room, pointing a finger at nobody in particular, although it's seemingly directed at the journalists from *L'Equipe*. 'You got your interview.'

As he walks out, I feel an unexpected flush of embarrassment – both for his boorish behaviour and for being British.

* * *

The next morning, in Bulle, waiting for the Garmin cars to arrive, I spot Nick Howes, at the foot of the steps of the Sky bus. When he thinks nobody's looking, he struggles to stifle a huge yawn.

'Late one, Nick?' I ask.

'They didn't turn the disco off until 2.30. And it was all that Euro rubbish – boom-boom-boom. But luckily the riders were at the back of the hotel so it wasn't that bad. Not for them anyway...'

It turned out that even after being shouted at, *L'Equipe* had still got their man, interviewing the recalcitrant Wiggins at the Hotel Callier the night before.

I spot the same Italian *commissaire* who'd exchanged words with Cavendish in the hotel foyer the evening before.

Cav's reputation, which he consistently argues is undeserved and unjustified, is that when the road goes uphill, he all too often hitches a 'ride' – by hanging on to wing mirrors – from a passing team car.

He's been accused of it in the past by other riders, as well as by the media. There is no damning evidence, though – just rumour and hearsay, all of which he has rubbished.

'Looks like they've got it in for him,' Sky's sports director Sean Yates says, referring to the *barrage* around Cavendish – the blockade imposed on team cars by UCI *commissaires* – at the foot of the final climb.

'They imposed the *barrage* 30 'k' from the finish and had three *commissaires* buzzing around Cav!' Yates says. 'I mean, three...!?'

A few minutes later, I stroll over to the Italian *commissaire* and shake hands.

'What was that about in the hotel last night with Cavendish?'

'We put some *commissaires* with Cavendish and he got a bit angry that we were there,' he shrugs. 'It's normal...'

Was he doing anything wrong, I ask – holding onto cars or anything like that?

'Oh no, no – nothing like that. But he's world champion, so a lot of people are watching him.'

An hour later, I climb into the passenger seat of Garmin's number one car, alongside Allan Peiper – white-haired these days, but still as thin as when he was racing. Peiper, once a team-mate of Yates and Robert Millar, then a *directeur sportif* to Cavendish and now to Garmin, is now something of a veteran.

Within a kilometre of the neutralised roll out, as Peiper and I renew acquaintance, we clip wing mirrors with another team car. Then the speed rises, up to 60 kilometres an hour as we slalom through the suburbs of Bulle.

I've been in team cars before – Motorola with Hennie Kuiper on the Tour of Britain, Festina with Juan Fernandez on the Tour de France – and now Peiper, but because Garmin's hot young talent Andrew Talansky is third overall, Peiper's number one team car is ranked third on the road. This means that we are constantly close to the back of the bunch.

Other than being on a motorbike, it is the best view of the peloton I have ever had.

Peiper, now a *directeur* for almost a decade, knows Cavendish well.

'In 10 years' time, this race will be famous for the world champion having worked for Wiggins. But then,' he adds, 'right now, Cav's in a good place.'

The attacks have already started, and Peiper urges his riders on through their radio earpieces: 'The boys are saying go, Ramunas,' he tells Garmin's Lithuanian rider, Ramunas Navardauskas.

The speed reaches 40 kilometres an hour uphill, 60 kilometres an hour on the flat, pushed along by the omnipresent, unrelenting Sky team, which chases down every move.

'Be ready guys, eh? Ready to go with the next ones,' Peiper tells them.

The valley narrows and closes in on the approach to the Col des Mosses. At the foot of the climb, as the gradient bites and the road swings through a beautiful wide hairpin, we pass Lotto rider Kenny Dehaes, bandaged and breathless, dropped on the first real incline. Peiper speaks to him in Flemish but we can both see that, with over 150 kilometres still to come, he's done for.

Other riders slide backwards towards us, scrabbling to hold on as Wiggins and Sky continue to force the pace. Cavendish is one of them, but he's fighting hard, with his race face on. Then, as much higher, snowy peaks come into view and Yates and Brailsford roll past in a Sky Jaguar, Peiper tucks into a sandwich, and there is a lull.

American Peter Stetina comes back to the car.

'It just wasn't happening,' he says to Peiper. 'Sky aren't letting anything go. Every time, it was just...' The Coloradan takes his hands off the bars and mimics a throttle being turned.

The top of the Col des Mosses is beautiful. Granite crags glower down on the peloton. Bright spring sunshine floods the Alpine meadows, still carpeted by crystallised snow, the road a ribbon of grey on the mountainside.

At the summit, Peiper speak to his riders again: 'Guys, it's a fast descent but make sure you're eating. It's a hard finale...'

'I'm surprised you have to remind them,' I say.

'Yeah, but they still forget sometimes – they get caught up in the race, then when they remember, it's already too late.'

We barrel down the descent, sometimes touching 90 kilometres per hour, pursuing the long line of riders, sweeping through the bends. High winds gust across the hillside and, as we slide through one left-hander, a BMC rider is gripping onto a blood spattered guardrail, left hand in the air, right hand clutching his face.

I check his race number.

'That's Van Garderen,' I say.

'Shit!' Peiper, his former directeur, exclaims. 'Was that TJ?'

We get to the valley floor and slalom through Aigle, within a stone's throw of the UCI's headquarters. As the race route turns into the valley towards Martigny, the peloton is met by a brutal headwind and the pace tumbles to 20 kilometres an hour.

With the bunch riding at a snail's pace, Peiper pulls over to the verge.

'I'm busting,' he says before jumping out and relieving himself. We move on. A BMC team car rolls alongside.

'TJ okay?' Peiper asks of BMC's Belgian *directeur*, Rik Verbrugghe.

'Yeah – he took a branch in the face, from a tree,' the Belgian says in clipped English.

Chris Froome appears alongside the Sky team car, and begins loading up with water bottles. I count six stuffed into his pockets and under his jersey, and two on his bike, before he rides back to the peloton.

The wind tugs at the hunched riders. Peiper and I chat some more and he praises the English affection for a cup of tea and a piece of cake.

'I like London,' he tells me. 'Last time I was there I ate at that Ramsay restaurant... What's it called? Petrus, that's the one. Impeccable it was.'

I suggest if he comes to London again that we combine Ramsay and a cuppa and should meet for tea in Claridge's.

'Aw, yeah – great idea!' he replies, as we shake on it.

Ryder Hesjedal drifts back for drinks and Alex The Mechanic begins worrying about how many more bidons the team needs.

'On a long, hot day we can get through 100,' he says, as he texts ahead to the 'ravito' – the *ravitaillement*, or feed zone – asking the soigneurs to prepare more bottles.

Sky are still working hard, riding relentlessly. Up ahead, Cavendish is battling the wind and leading the peloton as they begin to cut into the breakaway's lead. The time gap drops and then, as we arrive at the foot of a finishing circuit that includes two first-category climbs, Cav appears again, back alongside his team car.

'That's Cav's race,' Alex says as the world champion eases up and slips out of view behind the convoy. As we begin the first hairpins, Geraint Thomas – his work for Wiggins done – slips back, too. There's no need for a barrage this time. Within minutes both he and Cav are announced as abandons.

* * *

After the stage, on the way to the hotel, we take a detour and, on a whim, drive up the hairpins from Martigny, through the hanging vineyards, and up to the Col de Forclaz. There's one hotel and bar, so we park up, order a beer and take in the view.

A cyclo-tourist we passed on the way up the climb sweats over the top, zips up his jersey and promptly barrels through the first hairpin and into the descent. I watch him pass and, even though it's cold and getting dark, feel rather jealous and wonder where he's riding on to.

Wiggins was always expected to win the next day's decisive time trial. We hang around the Sky bus in the morning, chatting to the ever affable Howes, then drive the course before the race starts. There's a short uphill section, a quick steep descent, then a left turn onto a steady climb, cut into the mountainside that wends its way into Crans Montana.

In the press room – a school hall this time – the relaxed atmosphere of the race is emphasised by a sleepy and oversized Doberman lolling around in the entrance. Up at the finish line, the riders come and go – Cadel Evans, anonymous throughout the race, cutting a disconsolate figure as he crosses the line, still bereft of anything approaching real form.

Then, after Talansky, Peiper's protégé, rips up the course, it's time for Wiggins. The ever-watchful Brailsford monitors progress from the team camper van, parked 50 metres through the finish line. The Londoner pedals away from the start, flies down the descent but then grinds to a halt before the climb begins after his chain drops.

Marginal gains, marginal losses.

Wiggins fumbles with the bike very briefly, decides better of it, and then calmly stops. In the past he would have thrown the bike into a nearby ravine. This time, as the bike is substituted, he keeps his head, gets back on and sets off again.

He wins, if not easily from Talansky, but convincingly enough, the effort bringing him to near collapse as he crosses the line, cradled in Brailsford's arms. A few yards away, Peiper watches, a wry smile on his face, cursing Talansky's bad luck.

Half an hour later, Wiggins comes to the press room.

'I might be a knobhead with the press, but I'm consistent on the bike,' he says.

* * *

Modern cycling is all about context. The results have to be seen in the context of their time. Then, as time moves on, as cycling's history evolves, they become fluid, morphing as the landscape changes, becoming less credible – or sometimes more incredible – the more we learn and understand about each era.

So you could argue that Bradley Wiggins – as things stand finished second in the 2009 Tour de France. Take away Lance Armstrong's third place, Alberto Contador's win – both guided by Johan Bruyneel, of course – and bingo, Brad's runner-up.

The flipside is that immediately, of course, even

by finishing fourth, behind those infamous names, his performance put him under suspicion. Garmin, even as Wiggins prepared to walk out on Jonathan Vaughters' team in the aftermath of the 2009 Tour to join Team Sky, defended his reputation – and theirs.

Since then, his old *directeur*, Matt White – Whitey, to almost everyone in the peloton – has confessed to doping while employed as a US Postal rider. White was sacked by Garmin long after Wiggins's fourth place for sending a rider to see a doctor deemed dodgy because of his relations with Bruyneel and Armstrong, prior to Wiggins's fourth place.

At the end of 2012, White offered his resignation to the GreenEdge team after admitting to doping while he was on Armstrong's team.

Funny how it always comes back to Lance – the amazing Lance Armstrong. Amazing more in the way he managed to permeate almost every corner of cycling than for the 'incredible' results. Whitey rode with Lance, Whitey directs Brad, and Brad comes fourth in the Tour. Yates rode with Lance, Yates directs Brad, Brad wins. No wonder it makes some people nervous.

Of course, just because you know somebody with a reputation, it doesn't automatically mean that you deserve it, too. We all have friends with history, friends with reputations, damaged friends. Guilt by association does not stand up. But if you believe in it, as a signpost, then it's almost everywhere in cycling.

There's that word again – context: explain yourself, tell us what's really going on now, what really went on then. Tell us who you really are.

Perhaps, typically, we can lay much of the blame at Lance Armstrong's door, for his paranoia, his smokescreens, his bizarre and bitter Spanish tweeting from a pseudonym, his obsessions and his secrecy. Armstrong lived on his nerves, never relaxing, even during his downtime on the beach in Catalunya, watching his kids tuck into the *calamares romana*, while he picked irritably at a salad, and scrolled the messages on his BlackBerry.

Wiggins was never like this; his laid-back persona always seemed genuinely disconnected from the person he is on the bike. An Olympic pursuit is one thing, but how can somebody this outwardly relaxed, this simple in his world view, this happy nursing a pint in the corner of a pub, want to fight to win for three whole weeks?

Now, however, he seems the same: angry, defensive, berating the press, whether in the sleepy backwaters of the Tour of Romandy or the searing hothouse of the Tour de France.

How far removed in sentiment from Armstrong's extraordinary 'I'm sorry for the cynics and sceptics who don't believe in miracles' Hollywood moment on the podium at the end of the 2005 Tour was Wiggins's expletive-laden rant about Tweeters, seven summers later?

June 2012 in the Rhone Valley. Midway through the Critérium du Dauphiné. I'm driving through the pouring rain to Mont Brouilly, past more tumbling vineyards to Team Sky's hotel to interview Wiggins.

Bradley will do 10 minutes, says Nick Howes. 'About 8.15, okay?'

I'd asked for half an hour.

I wait in the dim and tiny reception area of the hotel. Tony Rominger, once a client of Michele Ferrari, mentor to a series of young riders, and now Cadel Evans's agent, wanders in and out of the lobby.

Wiggins comes past in kit, sheathed in sweat, his bib shorts rolled to his flat waist, rib cage protruding, skin white as a ghost, except for the tan lines above his elbows and around his neck. Not as tanned as others, though. He grunts an acknowledgement as he passes.

BMC directeur John Lelangue, once head of the Tour's press service, and son of Bob Lelangue, once a team-mate of Eddy Merckx, appears. Evans wanders through and down to dinner.

Rominger and Yates exchange a few words.

'Hey Sean, you still riding?' Rominger smiles. 'Look at you – so thin!'

'I don't eat much,' Yates replies.

An Italian TV crew arrives. Then the British documentary crew, who are following Sky through the year, settle in. I decide this is no place for an interview. Nick agrees and we move out into the car park and step onto the team bus.

Wiggins always sits at the front, Nick says. Or most of the time anyway. He gets on with the driver – they have a bit of a banter. I notice through the windows of the bus, blacked out from the outside, that he would always be able to survey the goings on around the bus.

'That makes me laugh, Nick,' I say. 'I can imagine them sitting here looking out at us, taking the piss.'

Nick smiles: 'Yeah, well, I won't say that never happens!'

Then Bradley appears, a little harassed, looking for a missing jacket. After a minute or two of searching, he sits down opposite me in his usual seat and we begin. I don't raise the issue of doping: he does.

'I'm only human. I get so upset about it,' he says, when I ask him about the rumours. 'My natural reaction is to want to tell somebody to go and fuck themselves. But you can't, 'cos they say, "Oh, what are you getting so touchy about...?" That's happening more and more and that's a shame. But I guess cycling has got itself to blame for it.'

We talk a little longer, but then, after just over 11 minutes, time is up. Nick's running a tight ship.

'Enjoy your dinner,' I say, as I pack away my notes, but he's already out of his seat, down the steps and gone.

I wait for the riders at the Sky bus after the next day's stage. Chris Froome warms down shaking his head and chatting to Mick Rogers. Both are relieved that they kept it all together for the finale.

Tim Kerrison, another of Sky's coaches and the one credited with revolutionising their thinking, stands watching. One by one he's handed the SRM system pods from each rider's bike. He stuffs them into the pocket of his team-issue hoodie.

I carry on down the line of buses and run into Charly Wegelius, outside the Garmin bus. Charly is writing a book, with the former rider Tom Southam.

'Another of our little collaborations,' he says with a wry smile, recalling the 2005 World Championships in Madrid, when Wegelius and Southam rode on the front of the bunch for several laps early in the race, helping the Italians rather than riding for Great Britain – a decision that cost national road coach John Herety his job.

We chat for a while, and he tells me how much he enjoys directing the team.

'I'm doing 100 days a year,' he explains. 'It really suits me; I love doing this. And I was ready to stop racing, really. I think I did one season too many.

'I'd always thought I'd handled it okay, but it wasn't until I stopped that I realised how tired I was, physically and mentally,' Charly says. 'I'd been exhausted most of the time.'

The next lunchtime I drive over the Joux Plane and on to Morzine. This is the acid test of Team Sky's pretensions, not just to win the Dauphiné, but the Tour. Brutal at the bottom and with enough tight hairpins to crack even the most determined *grimpeur*, it's worse than I remember it. The tarmac veers from smooth to ruptured and in places is washed by a mixture of mud and cow shit.

Over the top there's a corniche – stunning, with madly spectacular views – following a steep escarpment, another false summit and then a terrifying plunge through tall trees, down to Morzine.

Vertiginous isn't a word I use too often – in fact, it is – but it applies perfectly to the descent from the Joux Plane. Evans doesn't care and, still desperate to find his form, launches himself, first along the corniche and then down into the bends tumbling through the high pasture.

It's a spectacular attack, but it brings no response from Sky, who instead choose to let him go. Evans is risking his neck, but three weeks before the Tour starts, is it really worth it? Wiggins holds the lead and the race is effectively over.

There's a steep and rough path from the press room to the finish line. Nick Howes is wondering how Wiggins will get there.

'Can he ride down it?' he asks after the finish. In the end they drive.

Stage winner Nairo Quintana and Wiggins arrive in the press room at the same time. The tiny Colombian sits down, expressionless but attentive as the questions are asked. Wiggins stands to one side and looks slightly pained and awkward, but then with a shrug and smile sits down among the journalists as the South American responds.

Then it's Wiggins's turn, and somebody asks him if he thinks Sky race like US Postal.

'Yes, it's very similar to US Postal, and Banesto used to do the same thing. You race to your strengths as efficiently as possible. It works. We're not going to change it.'

Before I leave the press room, I remember something, and look up a recent quote from the UCI president Pat McQuaid, elaborating on the theme of the blood passport's success.

'For me, the evidence of the success of the passport seems on the road, in the race itself,' said McQuaid. 'I am not going to say that cycling has been winning the war against doping, but I will say that we have turned a corner on doping, and that the peloton is cleaner than it used to be.

'In the big mountain stages, you never see the [team] leader surrounded by three or four domestiques. He usually finishes the climb on his own. That wasn't the case during the big period of EPO,' said McQuaid.

Except that that is exactly what Wiggins and Team Sky did on the Joux Plane, in June 2012, as Cadel Evans toiled against them on his own. Four or five riders in black and sky blue set a searing pace and the bunch settled in behind them.

After I have read the USADA report, or most of it, I feel a need to go for a ride. It's Dave Zabriskie's testimony that resonates the most. Running from problems at home, from his father's addiction, he discovers cycling. It's a liberating experience for him. Then he turns professional and his dream sours. He finds himself in a hotel room, a bloody syringe in hand.

I feel polluted, blocked. I need to get out on the bike. The air gets colder on the road up from Sault, steadily climbing up through the forest. It's the forgotten side of Mont Ventoux, this old road, partly because it's less steep, wilder, and partly because it's not often used in races.

It's the loneliest side, too, and late on this October afternoon, 24 hours after I've stayed up most of the night, trawling through USADA's demolition of The Legend of Lance, it seems even more desolate.

I'm slow through the bends, painfully slow. I've spent too much time at a desk recently, so I churn, metronomically, through the bends that curl across the ploughed lavender fields and on up the gradient deep into the woods, the browned leaves gently falling onto the verge.

I hate the bastard Ventoux, because it's too hard for me, and always has been — but I love it, too. I've loved it since I first came up it in my mum's Mini Metro in 1986, wide-eyed and enthralled. The brakes seized on the way down and we ended up sliding into an exit lane, slewing through the gravel and sand as we plummeted towards Malaucène.

I love it even more now, on this chilly autumn afternoon. I love it for standing up to Lance the Bully, Lance the Fraud, Lance who thought he could have it all and get away with it, Lance who thought he was Untouchable. Well, he never 'had' the Ventoux, he never 'got' the Ventoux. It knew, you see – it knew who he really was. It had seen too much already, when Tom Simpson crossed its unforgiving slopes.

Finally the gradient eases – even though it's hardly that steep – and the road swings around to Chalet Reynard. I stop at the deserted café, lean the bike against the railings and down a café noisette on the terrace.

Lance came past here, many times, most famously with Marco Pantani. For a moment, in my mind's eye, I see them in tandem, wild-eyed, demented, doped up, haring past me on their way to the summit.

What did they signify as they skipped past and away, on up the mountain? Everything, everything, to the thousands of men, women and children who'd given up their time to come and stand and cheer at the roadside. Now, with Marco long gone and Lance found out, we know: it all meant nothing.

The wind picks up, the sky darkens and discretion gets the better part of valour. It's getting late. I won't be riding on to the top today.

It's suddenly icy cold and I pull on a second gilet before heading down to Bédoin, back home and to the warmth of a deep bath.

People used to say to Lance, 'What will be your legacy?'

Well, now we know.

Jeremy Whittle is cycling correspondent to *The Times*, author of *Bad Blood: The secret life of the Tour de France,*' and collaborator with David Millar on *Racing Through the Dark*. A founding editor of *procycling* magazine, he has written about sport, particularly European cycling, since 1994 and has covered 18 Tours de France.